To Tell the
TRUTH

Hope Beryl-Green

ISBN 978-1-64258-877-4 (paperback)
ISBN 978-1-64258-878-1 (digital)

Christian Faith Publishing, Inc.
832 Park Avenue
Meadville, PA 16335
www.christianfaithpublishing.com

Printed in the United States of America

Truth, at its essence, can be hard to hear, hard to believe and sometimes difficult to view. It can be confusing, mind-boggling and masked by the acts of evil. Evil so vile that it's easier to pretend that it doesn't exist, but it does. That is where the truth of Hope Beryl-Green's testimony shines. Denial can't erase it. Lies can't restrain it. What you're about to encounter is not only hard to read, it's difficult to accept. Human trafficking at the hands of satanic ritual abuse is a reality for some. The cries of the victims often go unheard or ignored. I thank God for Hope's courage to speak out against the lies and give voice to truth. Truth is what sets the captives free. I've watched Hope transform and heal because of pursuing truth through relationship with Jesus Christ. What you hold in your hands is a great and powerful work from His living-miracle Hope Beryl-Green.

—Michelle Chudy
#1 Bestselling Author, International Business Trainer
& Certified Coach, www.michellechudy.com

I have spent many hours with Hope working through the pain of her life story and programming. I can say without a shadow of a doubt that her story is to be believed and taken seriously. She is not lying. In fact, I believe she is a voice that speaks for more individuals than we are ready to accept. I applaud her bravery. This book will take you to the edge and back and force you to fundamentally shift the way you see this world. I pray that God takes this book far and wide!

—Daniel Duval, Executive Director of BRIDE Ministries

I've known Hope for some time now and have been blessed to be a part of her miraculous healing journey. Her testimony is unlike anything you may have ever heard and unfortunately more common than you may want to believe. Hope through her personal testimony reveals the horrifying depths of evil perpetrated against her and many others at the hands of her Illuminati abusers. But as much as her story reveals the evil of men it much more reveals the incredible goodness of God who rescued her from such bondage to the incredible freedom found in Christ Jesus. God is light and we who belong to Him love the light. But as light increases it also reveals what's been in the darkness and as we see what's been hidden in the darkness we can now cry out for justice. Honestly the contents of this book may deeply disturb you and it should but keep in mind it's only possible to know these things because Hope has been "…called out of darkness into his marvelous light" (1Peter 2:9b). I believe we are in a time of great awakening and I believe this book is for such a time such as this. I pray many many more victims will be delivered through the response to the revelations contained in this book.

—Joe Connelly, Missionary and
minister of the gospel of Jesus Christ

Chapter 1

Why I Share the Truth

"Then you will know the truth, and the
truth will set you free." John 8:32

This book was very difficult to write even though I lived it, so I know, without a doubt, it is difficult to hear and comprehend. But did you know that there are people in sex slavery, being tortured daily, government-funded mind control Illuminati victims? In this country, in your neighborhood, in your church? I'm sharing my story in great detail. Why am I sharing the truth in such depth? Because Jesus told me to tell the truth, and leave no detail out. Although it is difficult to fathom, it is essential to understanding the evil that is at work. There are millions of people who are slaves here in the United States, the land of the free. We have to stop looking at the outward appearance of a person, and walk by the Spirit. Walking by the Spirit would mean listening to the Spirit when we feel that something is just not right with a person. The disciples walked like this, the Spirit led them to call out people who were doing evil and pretending to be good. The disciples exposed these evil men and their true intentions. Jesus calls us to hate everything that God hates. Every disciple stood up against evil and many even lost their lives for speaking against it. Isaiah 5:20 says, "Woe to those who call evil good and good evil, who put darkness for light and light for darkness, who put bitter for sweet and sweet for bitter."

As the Church of Jesus, we need to allow people the freedom to tell the truth, and to expose the truth even if it's difficult to hear. People who talk about difficult things are labeled as negative, when they need to be encouraged to share the truth without fear of rejection. The Bible states that "The truth will set you free" (John 8:32).

Why tell people about the horrendous things that happened in my life? Because people are trying to distort, denigrate, defile, and pervert who Jesus is. The people who do these things pretend to be Christians, and they are getting away with it. They will ultimately be exposed at the end, because that is Papa God's promise in His Word. I believe He has called me to expose them now so that other people can be set free like me. These sons of Belial count on the Church, not being discerning enough to know they are in the midst of them. "For such men are false apostles, deceitful workers, disguising themselves as apostles of Christ. No wonder for even Satan disguises himself as an angel of light" (2 Corinthians 11:13–15). Jesus warned people of the false apostles and sons of Belial. If it was important enough for us to be warned about this in the Bible by Jesus, then why do we shy away from and act as though there is no need to see the truth of the evil and the slavery that is going on in the Church? Our highest calling is that we are supposed to be loving, if we are followers of Jesus, part of love is truth. Every darkness needs to be brought into the light. According to the Bible, in the end times, even the elect will be deceived. If we acknowledge the truth now and look into the light and the truth, we will not be deceived. William Wilberforce, an abolitionist, shared explicitly all of the details of the slavery that was going on in the world. He left no detail out, in his description of the horrors they were facing. He shared the putrid smell of evil, the abusive conditions that the slaves were kept in, and the horrors that they endured. "If to be feelingly alive to the sufferings of my fellow-creatures is to be a fanatic, I am one of the most incurable fanatics ever permitted to be at large" (William Wilberforce).

The truth was revealed by Wilberforce many years before people were willing to do anything about it. He continued on in the battle against slavery year after year, warring and battling with Papa God on his side, until finally the slaves were set free! Truth needs to be seen, in order to heal. It is imperative. Truth sets people free! For example, medicine tastes awful while its going down, but the end result of taking the medicine is healing. Just like Gianna Jensen, a survivor of a failed abortion, stated, "I didn't survive to make things comfortable. I survived to stir things up!" Jesus didn't tell people, "Sit back. I want everybody to be comfortable." He stirred things up! He didn't sit back and allow evil to prevail!

As we journey through my story, I pray that, as a wonderful lady I know once said, you will see "Papa God's story" in my story. That is my desire, and my prayer. There are a lot of things in my story that will not be easy to hear and will be hard to believe. That is understandable. We all wish that there wasn't evil in this world. But the reality is, we live in a fallen world, with a very real devil, that has no limit to the evil he is willing to do. For those that have chosen to follow Satan, they also have no limit to the evil that they are capable of. They have given themselves over to evil: body, mind, and spirit. They have made their choice to stand against Papa God, and they were not coerced to do so. By their own free will, they chose to serve Satan and do what he does.

I will share very candidly about my past. This is directly because the Lord asked me to do so. He told me not to hold anything back, to tell the truth in its entirety. This story needs to be told, and people need to hear. We are drawing to the end. We are being called to go speak truth and prepare the body of Christ so that we won't be caught off guard, with no idea of what is really going on in this world. Here is Papa God's cry to each of us: "Behold, I send My messenger before your face. Who will prepare Your Way before You. The voice of one crying in the wilderness; 'Prepare the way of the Lord; Make His paths straight'" (Mark 1:2).

Each of us, in our own individual unique way, prepare the way of the Lord. Papa God showed me that this is a "journey" for us. Journeys aren't meant to be fast. They are slow and detailed. Each minute, each moment means something. The journey is just as important as the finish. He gave me the analogy of a person getting in their car and stepping on the gas, going at top speed. They are full of anxiety and frustration that they aren't "there yet." But they are missing the lessons from the journey. In this fast-food culture, we really have to stand against that mind-set of the world. It causes us to miss out on so much that Papa God wants to show us. The devil tries to get us to think we won't be happy, we won't be good enough, we won't fulfill our destiny until we arrive at our destination—finally when one day our promises from Papa God are complete. But what if the journey is the purpose, and we miss the genuine message and joy He is trying to share with us now?

Let this book sink in page by page, chapter by chapter, until you get the full picture of what Papa God is trying to reveal. I will be sharing bits and pieces of what He is teaching me daily along the way while writing this book, as well as sharing the graphic details of my story and how I live each day now. After hearing about the hell that I survived, my life truly will be an expression of the power of Papa God to rescue anybody from anything! He is standing with His hand outstretched, waiting to walk through this with you, and I promise you will never be the same

Chapter 2

My Birth

"Before I formed you in the womb I knew you." Jeremiah 1:5

I was always suicidal from the earliest time I can remember. I hated being alive. I was filled with dread, fear, and constant torment of what would happen to me next. The people who programmed me made extremes so that if I ever told people what was going on, people would think I was crazy and say that I had a mental disorder. I had to create a false façade every day, every second, especially when we were around people. I acted like the programmers were perfect and we were a perfect family. If I ever let on that they were anything but perfect, they told me that I would never be allowed outside again. I was baffled as to why if I had the perfect family, why was I so horribly depressed, and why did I think I was the devil's child? Why did I constantly feel like there was something hideously evil inside of me that I could never get rid of?

It wasn't until I began falling apart and having flashbacks that Papa God began to show me the truth about my life. My mind had been deliberately programmed to forget all of my past and for me to live in a false reality to cover up what these people were doing to me. If you looked at us from the outside, we looked like the all-American family. This was a well-thought-out plan to cover up their evil actions, but most of all, the much bigger plan of the Illuminati in this country.

The lady who carried me in her womb was what the cult refers to as a "breeder" or "carrier." She was only existing to bring babies that had been dedicated to Satan and the Illuminati into this country. The people who brought me here were German. They have a German accent and speak German when they are not around people who could expose them. The lady programmer looked a lot like the lady who was carrying me. This was done on purpose to trick me and try to make me feel guilty about her death continually throughout my life when they were torturing me.

The Lord showed me clearly during my healing journey that I was put together in a petri dish, mixed with many different Illuminati bloodlines—specifically mixed with DNA from my programmers so that I would blend in with society by looking like them. According to human terms, I was put together specifically by evil men whose agenda was to have only one bloodline that they considered "the pure bloodline." *But Papa God!* He is ultimately the Creator of my blood and of my genetics! No matter how powerful the Illuminati is, they are no match for Papa God. I went through a time of intense sadness when Papa God revealed how they had mixed my DNA. The need to be a part of something, to be in a family, is a basic need of a human being. The programmers knew this, and they used this need against me every day. The lady who carried me in her womb was a victim. She was tortured and raped too. Papa God revealed this to me because I didn't understand why I had genuine love for her. He said that she loved me, and as an infant, I could feel the love that she had for me. Even in the womb, I was electrocuted by electric prods by the programmers. They would speak over me, "Die," "You are evil," "You are Satan's child." Scientifically, people would say that this is not possible to remember things from the womb, but Papa God can reveal anything He wants to bring healing. They killed this lady who carried me as I was being born and told me that it was my fault that she died. They said that if I ever got close to anyone, the same thing would happen to them.

The people who did this were German soldiers, and treated me like a prisoner of war. They hated anybody who was elderly, handicapped, Christians, Jews, anybody who was not in their elite group.

The infants that they chose to bring here were not in the elite group. We were told if we did what they said and helped them take down the Christians, then we were promised that we could live. We could be like them and be truly good, the perfect race. They told us that they were originally good, that they were the chosen people. The Illuminati would refer to themselves as the God in the garden and "we," the victims, were the ones who sinned. Therefore, we were evil, with an impure bloodline. In their narrative, Satan was trying to get us to be accepted by God, but God did not want to accept us as we were. Since we were the cause of all evil and were not perfect, God gave us to people who would torture us to be perfect like them. It was a horrible deception and hideous plan from Satan that the programmers deceived all victims to believe.

The Illuminati brought many infants into this country to train as German soldiers, who were planted into this society to accomplish a mission to take down America. The last time that was attempted. Hitler did it against the Jews. "On November 3, 1943, some forty-three thousand Jews were gathered, shot, and killed from various camps in Poland. This concluded Operation *Reinhard*, which had virtually exterminated Polish Jewry. The SS called this final action "Harvest Festival." While countless historians, commentators, and books have often emphasized the industrial nature of the holocaust, SS Nazis understood the concluding action of Operation *Reinhard* to be a special day on the farm comparable to an annual harvest celebration. In the twisted Nazi mind, Jewish weeds had to be eradicated from the blood and soil of Germany's *lebensraum*. Operation "Harvest Festival" was the single largest Nazi Jewish massacre conducted throughout the entire war. That is exactly what they are planning for Christians here in the United States, and for all of the victims ultimately. They used torture and mind control to make us believe we would be saved if we did what they told us to do.

This entire plan of the Illuminati is the attempt to destroy Christians. We were continually trained to fit into the Christian environment and tortured to take down the real Church slowly without them even knowing it. How is your biggest enemy defeated, they would say, "Catch them off guard, get them complacent, contented, believing all is well—so that when we attack there will be no retaliation, because it will be too late."

I remember being in a little cage as an infant. I was connected to a monitor that showed if my heart was beating or not. The rest of my body was covered with electrodes; wires were going everywhere. The programmers told me they were keeping me alive. When they showed me that my heart was beating on the monitor, they locked the cage. When they showed me that my heart wasn't beating on the monitor, they unlocked the cage. They would say over and over, "We determine if you live or die." If I moved, I was electrocuted. So they trained my every move to be only directed by them. I learned to stay still and only move when I was told to. When I would cry, I would be shocked, so I learned not to cry. I was then told over and over that I wasn't really hurting when I was in pain, that I shouldn't cry. And since I wasn't crying, they said, "You're not hurting." There was a constant state of confusion. The programmers would give me worms to eat and pretend like they were food. I had sores all over me from sitting in my feces and urine. When they would clean me up and put a diaper on me, they would be shocking my head at the same time. They would say over and over during the pain that I deserved the pain and that all of the pain was from God.

No matter what I did, they said I was wrong. I was put in a constant state of turmoil at all times. They would put a black cover over the cage that I was in and then tell me that I had died, and that I was alone. "God created you to torture you. He wants you here. He doesn't trust you. We have to torture you to be good enough." I was constantly thinking if I breathed right, moved right, maybe then they would let me out of this hell. They would say, "Be perfect as I am perfect. This is what God expects." No matter what, I couldn't be perfect enough. The programmers said they were born perfect, but I had to work for perfection. The programmers constantly said that God created me to never be good enough. The Illuminati say they are a divine race, that they are "perfect", and "gods." They would hook me up to a machine to reinforce what they were saying. This machine would shock me, and no matter how hard I worked, the pain never went away. So I worked harder and harder, and things never got better. I thought God hated me and wanted me to be in eternal pain.

In the hospital, I was put in a room with lots of other children. They were in cages too. Then I was put in a room by myself. I have no idea where I was; the room was white, sterile, and cold. I wasn't given food. I was given semen for food, to train me that having sex was my only way of survival. They were treating me like an animal. Actually, animals are treated better in this country than what I was treated.

At the same time, they were training me to attack like a soldier and training me to look perfect on the outside. The movie *Point of No Return* is the truth of what is done to many of the victims, except for those of us who have been brought there since birth. People see all of these movies today like *Conspiracy Theory*, and they think it is just fiction. It is real! I wish that people would ask themselves, "Where did they get the ideas for these movies?" The ideas are from rituals; it is in movies, because these things really do happen. The reason they have brought these movies out is they are trying to desensitize this country to the evil that is being perpetrated here. They are trying to make people in this country believe that nothing like that would ever happen. They told us that nobody would ever believe us and that they would think that we were crazy if we ever told. Another movie that shows the demonic foundation and territorial foundation of the Illuminati is the series of *Pirates of the Caribbean*. The octopus is a representation in rituals of all of the world leaders of Illuminati and their demonic power. The heart that is shown in the box in this movie represents the victims' heart in the ritual and how in the end times their heart will be exposed as evil. In the Satanic rituals, they cut out a human's heart and put it in a box. As victims, we are told if we choose to bury the truth about the Illuminati, they will not expose our heart as evil. This type of mind control and programming is foundational and is repeated over and over.

If you look at some of the people who go forward and share what happened to them, they are labeled as schizophrenic or paranoid. That's why the evil people did everything they could to try and make us feel like we were crazy. One of the biggest threats they made were that people would send us to a psychiatric hospital. What we knew of a hospital was the hell in the first five years of our life. We were brought up there, in seclusion, in torture. This ensured that we never told anybody, because we were too terrified to have to return to the hospital where we were programmed.

The programmers would poke my eyes with needles to cause my eyes to be red. Then they shaved my head and made me sit naked by myself in a room. They took pictures of me, and when I was forced to look at the pictures, they said, "See you even look like a demon." They made sure that I looked like a demon—with ribs sticking out, crouching on the floor, naked, deep red eyes, and a bald head—from all of the torture and deprivation. So when I saw myself in the mirror, I believed them when they said I was a hideous creature that deserved to be tortured.

What was their purpose in all this? To get me to believe at the core of who I was there was an evil monster who could not be trusted to be alone. An evil monster that deserved to be tortured. A demon that had been abandoned by God because of the wickedness of my heart. I knew nothing else other than what the programmers told me, so I believed their lies. That is how they controlled me. They programmed my mind to believe I needed them to control me. Without them, I thought that I was capable of no limit of evil.

As a child, I would fall asleep, and there would be a dead animal or dead person in the room with me when I woke up. They told me that I killed it while I was sleeping. I was terrified of myself. I hated being alone for terror that something evil within me would get out and do something horrible. They said God had given them the horrible task of keeping me from doing evil. I was tormented every moment, and there was no break from the torment. I lived with horrible guilt, shame, and terror of myself. I was glad that I was being tortured by them, because I was getting what I deserved. I wanted them to hurt me. I thought somehow it would make up for the evil things they said I had done.

As a child, I wasn't allowed to cry unless they said so. If I cried, they electrocuted me, and if I did cry, they would hurt someone and say it was my fault. I wasn't allowed to yawn, sneeze, go to the bathroom, eat, breathe without their say-so. When I was about three years old, they choked me until I was not able to breathe. I was gasping for breath. They said they gave me life and breath; without them, I wouldn't be able to live. They hooked me up to a heart monitor and told me that I had flatlined, that I had no heartbeat. Every person they brought in the room where I was at acted like I was dead. They began preparing me for the morgue. I was terrified as they were talking to each other. They talked like I wasn't there and said, "God hated her. He wanted her dead." Then the machine that they had me hooked up to started showing a heartbeat. They told me that they had brought me back, and God said that I could live if I let them hurt me and keep me under control. This was all before the age of five years old. They were laying a foundation of thinking that would keep me under their dominion.

A couple of days ago, I was sitting on our balcony with my husband, and there was a raccoon that was lying on the ground below us. I thought the raccoon was taking a nap, but Daniel said, "Hope, he will still be there at the end of the day." I felt intensely sad and responsible. So I started looking for a wildlife rescue in the area. I looked everywhere, and I couldn't find anybody. It was intense sadness that I was feeling. I couldn't help this poor raccoon. Then my mind went back to when I couldn't help the people who were dying in my arms. The many times that the people I tried to protect and wasn't allowed to protect. I couldn't save them. No matter what I did, I couldn't rescue them. Every single time, the evil people said it was my fault. The raccoon struggled to stand up and walk and then fell back down again. He was hurting, and it was tearing me up inside. I had watched so many people and animals suffer in my life I couldn't stand it. "What is going on, Lord? Why are You allowing this to happen?" I asked Papa God. He said, "To show you your heart. If your heart was evil, why would you care about that raccoon?" This was a profound moment that genuinely helped me see that I was not evil. Papa God can use even the smallest things in life to minister to us.

In a small amount of time, a buzzard began to try to get to the raccoon. I kept trying to scare it off, but it kept coming back. This brought back the hell I had lived through, of continually trying to protect people from getting devoured by buzzards. The people were killed by my programmers. They then told me their soul and spirit would be tormented forever if I let them be eaten by the birds or let the birds touch their body at all. I, once again, could not protect them. This is what I go through each day; there are triggers constantly. Triggers are programmed responses from sounds, smells, words, phrases, songs, hand gestures, and things throughout a normal day that would cause a response. These are established through horrific rituals and torture. I smell the smell of bubblegum, and I have flashbacks of the local doctor that was involved, raping me. I have the smell of vomit and have flashbacks of them allowing people to throw up on me and letting me sit in that horrid smell. Or the times, I would be left for days alone, with no food. Then they told me the only way I would survive was for me to eat the vomit.

There was a specific programmer who had a sign that he gave as a trigger. He didn't have a finger, so he would cut off a person's finger and shove it inside of my female parts. Then he said that he would always be a part of me and the other victims. So every time he showed the hand signal, it would remind me and the other victims what he had done to us, and start the terror all over again. A lot of Christian songs are used as triggers. For example, "Jesus, lover of my soul." The evil people raped me as they were singing that song. They dressed up like Jesus and held me down. "I will never let you go." "You have taken me from the miry clay, set my feet upon a rock, and now I know." The programmers put me in a dark hole by myself, and if I promised to pretend like they were perfect, I got to get out of the hole. But when I got out of the hole, I had to be raped. This abuse was done as the song was playing. So, when I was taken to church, I would hear the song and think that all Christians did those things. I thought everybody knew what I was going through, and they wanted me to get tortured, just like Jesus wanted me to be tortured. Every day, things were used as triggers to reinforce the programming. Coughing is another everyday thing that happens, but I was programmed about it. I was told that anybody who was coughing was trying to get people sick. Then when people got sick, the person was going to blame the sickness on me. They set this scenario

TO TELL THE TRUTH

up, and then they would torture me afterward. So they knew from then on that I would have extreme feelings of fear when someone coughed, and I would not trust them. In reality, every person that I would ever encounter would eventually cough, sneeze, or any of the tons of things they programmed me around; so this kept me chained to the evil people.

The evil people drugged me and told me that my hands and feet were like demons. They put fake claws on my hands and feet; then when I woke up from the drugs, I saw people who had been slashed up horribly, people who were completely torn apart. I was terrified because they told me I had been the person who killed them; I just didn't remember doing it. Since they showed me what I thought were my hands and feet that looked like claws, I was convinced I was an evil demonic monster. So from then on, I curled up my hands and place them under my armpits and curled up my toes too to keep people from seeing them and seeing who I really was. The programmers would curl up their arms or toes, and it was a sign to me that would trigger my mind to forget. An example of a smell trigger is the strong smell of egg. The male programmer was a college chemistry teacher. He had access to many different strong chemicals. He would use sulfur to burn people alive. This would melt their skin. Sulfur can even burn through rock. It also smells like eggs. I saw him burn people alive, with them screaming and crying for him to stop. The sulfur would be burning them, and the egg smell was there. Then, later to reinforce their torture, when they would make an egg sandwich, they would say they were going to burn me alive. This smell brings back horrible fear and pictures that are too excruciating to fathom. There are so many triggers that were created by the evil people I could write an entire book just about the triggers.

Chapter 3

The "Hospital"

"For there is nothing hidden that will not be disclosed,
and nothing concealed that will not be known or
brought out into the open." Luke 8:17

As I transition back to my story, I will share in detail the torture
that was done in the hospital that I was put in during the foundational years of zero to five. I was kept in a hospital setting with many
other children. I was tortured every moment of every day unless they
allowed me periodically to sleep. Even sleep was used as a means to
program me. They were constructing the foundational thinking of
my life that they wanted me to have so they could get away with all
of the torture, rape, and killing. They trained me like in the Pavlov
experiments, with the dog salivating at the sound of a bell. They
controlled me with shock torture, forcing me to have the behaviors
that they wanted. They employed specific programming to control
my every move, even training my brain to react the way they wanted
it to as well. Another type of Pavlov experiment that the programmers used on me was where they made me act like a dog. They made
me get on my hands and knees like a dog. Then they stimulated
my vagina, only when there were animals, children, or handicapped
people brought into the room. So this made me feel sexual feelings
at the most horrible times when those people were present. I hated
myself because I didn't want to feel sexual feelings when I saw them,

18

but they had stimulated me so that my body would react how they wanted it to. Then they said I was evil and disgusting because I had those sexual feelings.

The programmers would starve me and then make me fight for food like an animal. They used the scripture Mark 7:27, which says, "But Jesus said unto her, Let the children first be filled: for it is not good to take the children's bread, and to cast it unto the dogs." Then they would say since I was a mixed breed that I had to sit under their table and only eat the crumbs that fell from their table. Repeating over and over, they would say, "Jesus said you are a dog, so we are just treating you like He treats you." I genuinely thought, if Jesus says I'm a dog, then that must be what I will always be.

The programmers' objective was to control my every move and to make me think that I needed them to control me. A way they did this was by the process of pairing sexual feelings with unsexual things, then saying that I was evil for having sexual feelings. With causing sexual feelings continuously, they made me think I was evil and needed their control over me. This was used as just another way to trick me into thinking I was evil. They wanted me to hate myself so much that I would welcome the torture and the pain they were doing to me. In my mind, there was no other choice. I had to let them control me, or I would feel like an evil perverse monster.

Russian and German experiments that were "psychological" studies were actual rituals of torture, and they were used as torture techniques by the evil people. These type of "studies" started all of the basic triggers that would keep me under their control. There were thousands of code words that meant something different to victims than it would in the outside world. For example, when they said "God," I immediately thought of my "master" programmer. The male programmer also called himself my master, and he said he was my god. When the programmers said the name "Jesus," they were referring to the person they assigned to have sex with me. The person who was assigned the "Jesus" role was the only way I would get freedom, according to my programmers. Freedom meant to me that they would assign me a man to marry me that would control me every second, but I wouldn't have to be tortured. I will discuss this in more detail later in the book.

When the programmers said, "I'm praying for you," that meant that they were killing people for me. To pray meant "to prey," to do horrible things to people. The programmers would get down on their knees and say they were "preying." I knew that meant someone was going to get hurt horribly or killed. They said they were killing people for me because I was evil. I needed a sacrifice to be good enough since the Jesus of the church didn't choose me.

I was tortured as a child around each main color. I was programmed that when I saw that color or I wore that color, I was to allow a different part of my mind or alter to be out. Red meant sex parts were out. These were the parts or alters that were trained to have sex. The sex parts would have to be present and have sex with whomever the programmers said whenever they said. White meant the "God and Jesus" parts had to be out. The "God and Jesus" parts had to be perfect and were forced to be judge and determine who lived or died. The programmers made these parts think that they had a choice, but there was never a choice. For example, "You can allow one of these two people to live or die." There was never a good choice offered; my heart was ripped to shreds. Black meant the evil and death parts had to be present. Everywhere those parts of my mind went, something evil happened, and someone died, and the programmers manipulated these parts such that I'd be tricked into believing it was always my fault. Navy meant royalty parts were forced to perform. The royalty parts had been given false kingdoms and titles to cause a false pride. If you are completely deprived of all self-worth, you will do anything for purpose and meaning—anything to make you feel important somewhere, somehow. These titles and kingdoms were only given if I took on the demons that were over them. Purple meant Illuminati parts were to perform. This color meant that the Illuminati ruled and reigned over me, and I was their product. Anytime a programmer wears purple, that means that they are showing off their merchandise and product that day, and I knew I would be sold in an auction that day. Purple was a reminder that I was not free and that they owned me. This was reinforced in rituals by the Scripture "I am not my own, I have been bought with a price" (1 Corinthians 6:19–20). Pink meant princess pretend alters were out. The denial parts of my mind were forced to pretend that the programmers were perfect parents. This was normally when we were out in public. The color gold meant number one in the Illuminati. The right side of the brain and body was in charge when the alters were out, and that part of my brain and body had to take control. The color silver, number two, meant the left side of the brain and body alters were out. So in summary, the left side was the evil side, and the right side was the good side in my programming. This was also reinforced through Scripture: Jesus was always at the right hand of the Father. And the right hand was seen as holy, while the left hand was seen as defiled. They programmed me to believe that I had to be number one at all times out in public in order to earn my husband, who was going to control me. This programming was done in such great detail that whatever underwear I wore meant what part was out, and what outfit meant what I had to do that day. These colors are used in rituals and are programmed down to even how they choose the car you drive. There was an underlying reason for every single thing that they did. The main reason they go to such great detail in their programming is that ensures that no person will even suspect that they are doing evil; it is a devious setup against the victims. All of their communication is hidden, appearing even "Christian," but underneath there is a much different meaning to what they are doing.

The programmers put *Wizard of Oz* programming in place in the first five years of my life. If you look around you on a daily basis, there are so many phrases from that movie that are spoken in everyday life. If you research the *Wizard of Oz*, you will see its Satanic roots. They would set up rituals where God was the mayor of Oz; and he decided who got a heart, a brain, courage, etc. If we didn't get these "gifts," we were supposed to play the role of someone who was lacking in those areas. The entire goal was that we played a character like Dorothy was in the dream. We had to pretend we were dreaming all of the bad things that were happening. The evil people said that the yellow brick road was the road to heaven, so if I pretended well enough, I would get to go to heaven. But I never was good enough. They continually tried to cause competition between the victims, and if we weren't chosen, then the wedding feast meant our death. They tried to create a denial world in my mind and in every situation so that as we got into the society, no one would suspect that we were being hurt.

After the first five years of my life, it was time to move me into society. They chose a small town in Kentucky that was of German decent. It was the name of a German city in the Third Reich. They would blend me into the society there and cause the people to never think that they could ever hurt "their child." They enrolled me into the local school. The male programmer was a teacher, a coach, and a counselor in the school. So he was able to be there to control my every move. He made sure that he put me where there were other victims or programmers. And if someone spoke to me outside of the people who were allowed to speak to me, then he tried to discredit them by saying to me that they were part of why I was there. My programmers would go on to say the person knew how evil I was, and they were just playing the game too.

The programmers put me in the doghouse behind their house a lot. He built a doghouse that had a pen and a back shed that had a bolt on it. It was covered over with a piece of wood, and they kept me in it with the dog. They had a heat lamp they said was for the dog to stay warm. I didn't deserve to be warm, they said. The reality was that I had to sleep with the dog, which was my only interaction in life for long periods of time. I would grow to love the dog and to cling to it. When they saw that I loved the dog, they would kill it and say it was my fault. I had no one. I was completely alone.

I don't share all of this for the shock and awe value. I share this because Papa God has told me to share these details. Luke 8:17 says, "For there is nothing hidden that will not be disclosed and nothing concealed that will not be known or brought out into the open." Papa God wants all of the evil things done by evil people to be exposed. Bringing things into the light brings healing. First John 1:15 says, "God is the Light; in Him there is no darkness at all." He doesn't just ask us to be honest about the highlights of our life but also the darkness so that people can be made aware. How can a person be rescued if no one knows they are enslaved? I was treated like an animal, led around like a dog with a leash. They would blow a whistle, and that meant all of the dogs (mixed breed victims) had to gather together. My programmers said that *God* was *dog* spelled backward, so since I wasn't God or His chosen child, then I was a dog, the very opposite of God. They forced me to get on my hands and knees and repent to them for being so evil.

Chapter 4

Sharing the Truth

"You who are full of all deceit and fraud, you son of the
devil, you enemy of all righteousness, will you not cease to
make crooked the straight ways of the Lord?" Acts 13:10

The other day on the way to the gym, I was behind a garbage
truck. I was annoyed because the truck was slowing me down. Papa
God told me to look at that garbage truck. Repenting is like that
garbage truck. Repenting is not saying you're evil or a piece of trash.
Repenting is to allow us to take all of the trash, the sin, that keep
us from seeing who we really are—completely away. Repenting is
actually revealing we're beautiful children of God. Papa God never
meant for us to believe that we are trash because we made a mistake.
We tell Papa God about the sin that needs to be taken away, and He
gathers it up and takes it away. So we are left with a clean house, free
to be free!

Jesus warns us about evil people throughout Scripture. He
speaks in Romans about giving them over to a debased mind, filled
with all unrighteousness, vile passions, murder, evil-mindedness, and
the list goes on. Romans 1:28–30 says, "Furthermore, just as they did
not think it worthwhile to retain the knowledge of God, so God gave
them over to a depraved mind, so that they do what ought not to be
done. They have become filled with every kind of wickedness, evil,
greed and depravity. They are full of envy, murder, strife, deceit and

malice. They are gossips, slanderers, God-haters, insolent, arrogant and boastful; they invent ways of doing evil."

Papa God also shares that they know who God is but choose to do these things. They pretend to detest the people who are doing the very evil things they do. This is the reason Papa God warns us not to look at the surface of a person, to discern with the Holy Spirit. All things that look good are not always good. I was very confused many times because Christians would shame me and say I needed to pray for them. As I began to ask Papa God about praying for the programmers, the very next day, He revealed in Scripture my answer that confirmed that I should not pray for them. Jeremiah 7:16 says, "So do not pray for this people nor offer any plea or petition for them; do not plead with me, for I will not listen to you." Only because of the evil people's willful choice to give their entire creation over to Satan. They didn't choose what they chose because of wounds or pain. They chose Satan while being fully aware of who Papa God is and about Jesus's death and resurrection. They actually know more about Scripture than most Christians do, because they twist and pervert every Scripture.

The people who hurt me were schoolteachers, a deacon, and a women's leader in the local Baptist church. This is where the Illuminati and sex traffickers hide. They hide so they can divide and conquer. The enemy has tricked us into judging by what we see on the outside, instead of judging by the Spirit. The Spirit leads us into true judgment. Jesus warned us over and over again that there would be people who would appear good and would be evil.

Second Corinthians 11:13–15 says, "For such men are false apostles, deceitful workers, disguising themselves as apostles of Christ. No wonder, for even Satan disguises himself as an angel of light. Therefore, it is not surprising if his servants also disguise themselves as servants of righteousness, whose end will be according to their deeds." The definition of *disguise* is to give (someone or oneself) a different appearance in order to conceal one's identity, pass oneself off as impersonate. They do all of this willfully without any form of remorse.

The place where the evil people kept the victims had a morgue; at the time, of course, I didn't know what it was. They would put us in the drawers and not let us out. The dead people were already decomposing; sometimes they would put us in the drawers with parts of the bodies. This was horrifying. They told us that God had sent us to hell—that if we didn't do what God told us to do, we would have to stay there. The only way out of hell was to kill someone. If we killed them, they told us that we would get to live and the person who was dead would come back to life and not have to stay there. This was to reinforce in us that Jesus did not die for us, that we were too bad, and that we had to have another sacrifice for us to not go to hell. I never ever chose to hurt anybody, not once. I was forced physically, mentally, and emotionally. That was the worst part of all of the torture because that went against who I was as a child of Papa God.

The people were already dead in the cold chambers in the morgue, but to a three-year-old, there was no difference. So each of us had to stab a person. They took the knife in our hand and made us do it. Then stood back and said, "You are so evil. God hates you. Look what you did. You killed this person." I asked when the person was going to wake up, like they promised us would happen; but the person never woke up.

So all of the other victims and I were programmed that we were evil and we kill people. Then the evil people used this and would reinforce that we needed them because they would keep us from doing evil. We believed them. There is no greater hell than to think that no matter what you do you will never be good, never be able to trust yourself, and there is a deep torment and torture to your soul and spirit. This is the deepest core lie that the Illuminati built on over and over again. They called me the "master executioner," "*me*."

This torture still affects me to this day. I always second-guess myself. Even if I genuinely know I haven't done anything wrong, I look for an evil motive inside as to why I do something. I don't trust that I deserve to be treated in a kind way. Someone I love walked in the door last night, and I sensed something was wrong, and I asked them if there was something wrong. They got offended and began to get angry and yell at me. Instead of taking up for myself, I just took the yelling. I didn't require them to treat me differently. They trained me to be a doormat, to never stand up for myself. Why should I ask to be treated kindly? The programmers said I was evil; I had no rights.

The other day, I was listening to the radio about Christian writers. They said that beauty and truth are the two main reasons for writing. They went on to say that the truth is not what people flock to because it's difficult to hear, but it's just as important. I choose to write the truth even if no one chooses to hear, even if no one listens. There are millions of slaves out there in this country that I write this book for—for those that have no voice and no way out. Wait, I promise there is Someone that is on His *way* to rescue you, and He is bringing all of His children who say *yes* with Him! I care, and I will stand for you!

Each of you are called for such a time as this, to rescue those that Papa God is calling you to rescue. You are taking a huge first step, arming yourself with the truth you need to be aware of, the reality of what you are facing. I was so angry that I had to wait thirty years to be set free. I cried out and asked Papa God why He didn't rescue me sooner. He said, "I asked thousands of people, Hope, to reach out to you, to listen and see the truth, but they did not." You could be the person whom someone has been waiting for their entire lives, someone who will see the truth, and be a way out for them! As I transition back to my story, ask Papa God if there is any way you can help. What is your piece to the puzzle of freedom for somebody? There is no piece too small or too insignificant.

A common way they reinforced the thinking that I was evil is taking pictures with me doing things they had forced me to do, but in the picture, it did not look forced. They would use the pictures as leverage. "Don't ever tell anybody, or we will take these pictures to the police." All of the victims hated the thought of jail because they had told us that it was just like the hell we started out in. They said we would be tortured there and never get out.

It's Halloween as I'm writing this. The night of the 30th after midnight is the worst time of sacrifice and rituals. The programmers say they determine who gets to go to heaven and who gets to go to hell. There is a huge corporate ritual with powerful people from all walks of life—doctors, lawyers, teachers, pastors, judges. As a victim, you get evaluated and tested for the whole year by the Illuminati on how well you did to accomplish their plans. The two options that were given were to go to hell and realize how evil you really are, to be the evil person that God created you to be forever; or go to heaven. In heaven, the torture is all the same, but you pretend like it isn't. If you pretend well enough, you get another year to try and be good enough.

A lot of this is based on programming from the *Wizard of Oz*. You go to the emerald city and get a new brain, heart, etc.; and you go out and pretend that things are perfect. If you do this well enough, the evil people say that you never will have to go to hell. Of course, all of this is a lie. The same torture and terror continues everywhere with the evil people. They are continually building a denial system to cover up what they do to us.

The corporate rituals continue until November 5, election day. They chose election day because it's their way of reinforcing to victims that they are not in the "elect class." The evil people say that they are the elite, the elect, that are chosen by god, but their god is Satan. The Illuminati's plan and destiny, according to them, is to destroy those that are not "elect." They have been for decades and currently are making an army of trained tortured slaves that are set in place in every city throughout the world—people who are like me, who were born into the Illuminati with the programming and torture. We are told if we do our job, then we can become the "elect," and we will be set free. At that time, we won't be evil anymore. Every single aspect of a victim's life is a double bind. Every time you try to cause the least damage or pain, it is turned and used against you.

The school shootings and the random shootings you have seen are in majority people who have been programmed to do that job. I have seen maps of the United States, and the targets of each state, and their ultimate goal for that state. They continually said, "We are going to take over the US, and our trained army and terrorists are going to help us do that." Just like Hitler tried to take over the world, that is how they are going about destroying us within, bit by bit taking down the United States.

A way that this plan is slightly different than Hitler's plan is that the Illuminati is hiding their every move and waiting until the day all of the steps have been carried out. That way, they will catch the United States off guard and unaware that there even was a plan to take over. Satan works as an angel of light, deceiving people into believing he is good and then trapping them. The best prey is the prey that has no idea that they are even being attacked.

The list of the ways that the evil people have tried to destroy my life are endless. I get up this morning, and I feel anger and rage. The programmers continually would not let me sleep. I would sleep maybe two hours after the rituals. Then they would say, "You have to get up and spend time with god." This meant that I had to get up and get on my knees and get raped by god to make me better.

The person who raped me was a person who had the god title. The programmers would say they were sent to be god for me on earth. They were sent to keep me in line. "In line" had a hidden meaning; it meant that I died, "flatlined," and they took over. They would hook me up to a heart monitor to reinforce this ritual. The monitor would show a heartbeat, and the evil people would say, "You better let us take control of your heart, or something bad will happen." If I did what they told me to, then my heart would be under their control. Like an animal, they gave me commands, and I had to do them. Sit, speak, roll over (get raped), go to the bathroom (I couldn't go unless they said I could).

I would be on display like a science project when they would have their corporate rituals. All of the programmers would display their "work." There were times when I would wake up, and the evil people would say, "What did you do!" There would be someone whom they killed in their ritual that night, and they would say, "You did this during the night. Your heart wasn't under our control!" So I believed that I was wicked and evil, and that I could not trust myself. I wanted to be controlled because I was afraid of myself. The reality was that I never killed anybody, but I didn't know any different about myself.

I never thought I would ever get any justice on this earth due to the fact that they cover their tracks so well. They have people watching out for them continuously to make sure that there is no one following them or anyone close to where they are who could hear, see, or find out anything. They also dispatch demons to cover their tracks and to cause confusion in the spirit realm so that people will not be able to discern anything about them. They summon demons to cause a trancelike state in people as they talk to them. This causes a wall of denial and numbness to fall on the person. The demonics block the Holy Spirit from exposing their true identity. People need to be aware so that they can combat these demonics and walk in the freedom that is theirs. Powerful Illuminati leaders request for corporate demonic powers to come over the minds of people when listening to them speak on TV or at conferences. If the person listens to these top Illuminati leaders who are positioned throughout our culture, in media, entertainment, politics, sports, etc. Eventually, the person will no longer see anything other than what the Illuminati leader is wanting them to see; all of the evil will be disguised by demonic trances. They will no longer think that that person can do any wrong and begin to idolize them. At the rituals, the more innocent blood is shed, the more power the Illuminati receives. These sacrifices also give the programmers more power so that they can be taken over by the demons to be able to embody what they are trying to get people to see them as.

At the corporate rituals, each controller is showing off his programming and trying to find new ways to control their victims. The Illuminati study the way the brain works with experiments being carried out on the brain every day. They try to continually come up with ways to gain more control of the victims and over the people in this country.

Our spirits cannot be controlled, though! They could not make me choose Satan! They could not make me be evil! The spirit is the strongest area of our being. The Lord showed me that He protected my spirit. I chose Papa God, and there was not a thing the evil people could do about it.

Chapter 5

This is Real

"You are of your father the devil, and you want to do the desires of your father. He was a murderer from the beginning, and does not stand in the truth because there is no truth in him. Whenever he speaks a lie, he speaks from his own nature, for he is a liar and the father of lies." John 8:44

Papa God had me read John 9 today. When Jesus spat on the ground, He was prophesying that His life was going to the ground in death. He would heal us and bring us out of the curse. His life brings complete healing. The pool of Siloam means "sent." Jesus was sent to wash away all of our wounds and to heal us completely, to bring us spiritual sight. "I once was blind, but now I see!" He washes us with the *truth*. The truth is imperative. In John 9:6, it states, "When He had said these things, He spat on the ground and made clay with the saliva." Jesus spoke the truth that the blind man was not blind because of any sin of his or his parents. Papa God is showing that His DNA is what is causing the healing. His DNA brings life; He brings life. The flesh and sickness were cancelled. The life of Jesus (saliva) brought healing and truth to the blind man. Then Jesus had the man go and wash in the pool of Siloam (sent). This represents Jesus being sent to wash away our sins, the fall of man from the perfect creation that we were made to be by Papa God. Also, this represents the way that Jesus heals us and sends us out to share with others how He has healed us.

As I shared earlier, the evil people say that there are two types of humans, the perfect humans and the imperfect. The imperfect were made out of dirt by God, and the perfect humans are written about in a different book that says that they are the chosen people. They were not created. They are gods with Satan; he is their leader. According to them, God is trying to take them down because He knows that they are more powerful than He is. I was told that the "real god," Satan, doesn't make dirt like God does. Since we are made from dirt, God made an inferior creature on purpose to control. The programmers said that is why they controlled me. They said over and over that God said we needed to be controlled.

The Illuminati says that they are equal to God and Satan. They believe they will rule together as soon as they get rid of the inferior race. So that is why they have put together an army all over the world that is programmed to exterminate all those that are not Illuminati; this army is in place to dominate and control the world and destroy those who do not comply.

The majority of their trained soldiers are innocent victims who have been programmed to complete a mission so that they can be good enough to go to heaven (be the chosen few who are a perfect race). Just like Muslims teach, you can be grafted in if they take out enough of the inferior race, the Christians.

There is a very strong connection with the Muslim jihad and the Illuminati. They both are wanting the same outcome. The Illuminati and the Muslim jihad are partnered together to help each other destroy Christians. The Illuminati funds the ISIS and the jihad. I have seen many jihad at the rituals, celebrating that they massacred Christians. They celebrate because Satan gives them more power to complete their missions. They use witchcraft and sorcery to cover their tracks, to sneak onto planes and into places where they are planning attacks.

Many of the jihadists are being trained by some of our military: tactics of war and mind control. How do I know this? Because I was a victim of their tactics. There were many Muslim jihad members who came to the Illuminati to learn the secrets they have, to destroy Christians. There is a very big picture here, a picture that is unfolding right before our eyes; and the majority of people have no idea what is happening. My programmers said that there would be an Aryan man who would be raised up. He would pretend like he was Christian, but like Hitler, his ultimate goal would be to annihilate those who aren't of the Aryan race.

Despite all of this, I do not fear, because I know the end of the story: Jesus wins! We win! I do think that the Lord has called us to be aware of the enemies' strategies so we can be successful in rescuing innocent victims and be the type of people who are on the offense, not the defense. We are God's children; Satan's powers are nonexistent compared to God's. Unfortunately, if we are not aware of Satan's tactics, we run the risk of being caught off guard and end up on the defensive. For example, the quarterback is the man in charge in football. He has the ability to win the game with help from his teammates. In order to be successful and keep from being beat up in the process, they have a strategy.

Another way the Illuminati completes their purpose is to blend into the culture. The people who tortured, raped, and programmed me were teachers in the local school they sent me to. He was a teacher, a counselor, basketball coach, softball coach, and track coach. He was involved in every detail of my life, every second. He did not allow me to be alone with anyone other than whom he said I could be around. If someone happened to speak to me who was not someone he allowed, he would tell me later, "They know how evil you are. They are just testing you to see if you will mess up. They were checking you out so they could buy you." So I never trusted any person, and I thought this was normal life. I just thought every person knew what was happening to me, and they agreed that it should happen.

My female programmer was a head start teacher. The person she called her sister worked at the board of education. She made sure all of my files were taken care of and no one found out about them. Both of the programmers were very involved in the Baptist Church there to keep their cover and make them look like the "perfect family." He was a deacon, and she was over the kids' church. They hid the "hell" I lived in, very well. They called in demons to cover them daily. The demons gave them the power to be the embodiment of what they are trying to represent. They also, cloak themselves in demons so that people will never discern that they are not what they present themselves to be.

Large rituals are done corporately to call in demons into the church or wherever they are trying to infiltrate to cause confusion and division. So if you feel confusion constantly when you're around someone, ask Papa God, "Why do I feel confusion?" I think the enemy has tried to get the church to a place where they do not question their feelings or spirit. When they see something that looks good, they take that at face value.

The culture teaches people to be polite, to be nice, to not question things. There were many times that Jesus and the disciples were not "nice" in our culture's meaning of the word *nice*. Jesus and the disciples discerned and called out evil. They exposed a person when they were inwardly something different from what they were presenting outwardly. They had to rely on what the Holy Spirit was telling them, not what they were seeing. Matthew 3:7 says, "But when he saw many of the Pharisees and Sadducees coming to where he was baptizing, he said to them: 'You brood of vipers! Who warned you to flee from the coming wrath?'" I cry out for a spirit of discernment for the church.

Ephesians 3:10 says, "His intent was that now, through the church, the manifold wisdom of God should be made known to the rulers and authorities in the heavenly realms." We need discernment and wisdom in the church! The concentration camps and the people who are building them and funding them need to be exposed. The atrocities that are happening to innocent people who are living in a continual hell that is not a choice of their own needs to be exposed! I pray the church will be awake to all that is happening around them and within their walls.

The effect of the horrendous torture and programming I went through still affects me daily, all throughout the day. When I least expect it, a trigger happens, and I have to deal with flashbacks and the pain of the horror I went through. Where I live currently, lately, there have been tons of buzzards, at least fifty or more, around my apartment. There is a waterfall close to where we live, and many trees. The buzzards are everywhere! This gives me a very uneasy feeling. Anytime there were buzzards around in my life, it meant somebody had been killed, and it meant that as the lowest level of humanity (that's what the evil people called me), I would have to see the people ripped apart by buzzards, and they would make me eat the remains. I would throw up over and over, but no matter what, I had to finish whatever they said to finish. They said that I had killed the person during the night, and I had to get rid of the evidence. They were "just protecting me," they said. I begged to die. I begged to be killed; but they said if I died, I would be completely out of control, and a lot more people would die. So even suicide was not an option. I didn't want anybody to die, and I didn't want to be completely evil. So there was no way out for me. I was forced to do what they said every second of every day. I have asked many, many times, "Why, Papa God? Why haven't You exposed the evil people? Why haven't You made them pay for what they did and are continuing to do?" His response has always been, "I do not want to take down the innocent people with the evil people, I will not hurt my children." This is reflected in Scripture, Romans 9:22–24. "What if God, wanting to show His wrath and to make His power known, endured with much longsuffering the vessels of wrath prepared for destruction, that He might make known the riches of His glory on the vessels of mercy, which He had prepared beforehand for glory."

During all of the programming, they had paired me with another female victim. We were supposed to be best friends, as far as anybody knew in our day-to-day life. But in reality, they tortured us against each other. They tortured me to hate her, and tortured her to hate me. We had to compete with each other, constantly. We were around five or six years old, and we began to go to gymnastics together. They had a programmer that was our "coach." They dressed us alike and did our hair the same so we would constantly see who looked and acted the best. If she won, I was tortured, and if I won, she was tor-tured. We were trained to blame each other. They bonded us through pain and torture. They trained her to be the dominant one, and me to be the underdog. That was our programmed roles in the cult. The dominant one had to torture the underdog into submission. In the rituals, the dominant one put a leash on the underdog and told them what to do. If the underdog did not do everything right, they would get tortured. The cult gives the dominant victim a false sense of control. They feel guilt and shame for torturing their "friend," but they are also told that the underdog will turn on people and do horrible things, so it's their job to make sure that doesn't happen. The underdogs have a leash put on us, and we are tortured in submission. We are told not to not make a move unless we are told. So we feel an extreme need to be controlled because we have been told that we are an evil animal that needs to be stopped. Our programmers dressed us up just alike and said we were sisters.

I feel dread and pain as I begin to write, even as I think about writing. There are so many emotions that I have bottled up from trying to survive over the years. I have not wanted to feel a lot of the emotions of today, because I needed to stay focused on healing of my past. The truth is that I was hideously tortured and raped my entire life. There are countless ways this continues to affect my life. My marriage is affected because I was controlled and never given the option of making my own choices. So today when my husband asks me what I would like to do or where I would like to eat, etc., I have difficulty expressing myself and giving any input. My physical body was always worn down and tired, and this still affects me today.

I have been healed so much in my mind, spirit, and body throughout this journey. Papa God began to show me that I have power within me; it's not true that I can't do things. I can do anything I want because I have the power of Papa God and the entire kingdom of heaven within me. I began to sing, "I have power in the name of Jesus. I have power in the name of Jesus. I have power in the name of Jesus to break every chain!" While singing this one day, Jesus showed me a vision of all of heaven rejoicing when I sang that and saying, "Finally, she sees the truth." I think Papa God rejoices when we see the power we have been given. The church, unfortunately, sometimes teaches that we can get prideful easily and that we should focus on the thought that we can't do anything and that we are useless. The reality is we can do anything with Jesus! He doesn't want us to sit around and say, "Well, I will wait till Papa God does this." He already has, and He has already empowered us. He already gave us the power of heaven! I went to work the same day that Jesus revealed this to me, and had the attitude of "I can do this. I'm powerful!" Throughout the day, I resolved issues and engaged in a way that I had never experienced. I was excelling. Later in the day, my heart was hurting horribly. I have had this happen before, but I wasn't sure the reason behind the intense pain. Papa God revealed to me the root cause of why I was having the chest pain. The programmers had told me that my heart would explode if I made any of my own choices, that it would blow up because of the evil inside of me. They said I wouldn't be able to go to heaven, because I wouldn't have a heart that could be saved. The evil people had tortured me and tortured other people in front of me to believe this lie. They said that if I ever made my own choices, I would cause them to die. It would be my fault for choosing something on my own, without being under their control. Papa God showed me that the reality is, I can make my own choices now. I can choose anything anytime I want. It's not bad to make my own choices. I can be trusted. I'm not evil. I see each day the truth that I can genuinely make my own choices. This is what abundant life is all about! I have talked to many people who wonder why Papa God gave us free will because we end up making so many bad choices. The deepest unconditional love is to allow a person the freedom to choose! Without choice, this is not living. We are just robots that do what our master controls us to do! After being a slave for thirty years, I see the absolute love that Papa God has for us in that He gave us the freedom to choose the life we want, the freedom to choose Him. He will not force us to choose Him, He will show us in every possible way who He is and His love for us, but the final choice is ours. We can choose God and heaven, or Satan and hell. Abundant life or death—it's our choice. We are not robots and slaves who are forced to be what He wants us to be or do what He wants us to do. Please take it from someone who was a slave for thirty years. There is no love in that, in any way, shape, or form, captivity is hell continuously!

In Matthew 10:39, it says, "Whoever finds their life will lose it, and whoever loses their life for my sake will find it." This scripture was used to torture me and control my mind. Along with many other scriptures, the evil people twisted them to mean what they wanted them to mean. The evil people said that I had to lose my life. This meant that I had to do everything that they told me to. If I found my life, if I made my own choices, then I would lose my life. Losing my life meant that God showed up and took everything away from me. So I was constantly in fear of making any choices of my own. I refused to make choices, and I was tortured to never make choices. They would say, "Find your life!" At that time, they would torture someone or something that they had briefly allowed me to get close to. Then they would say, "God made you lose your life because you are evil and make people suffer." So I was afraid of having a life and choices because that meant something very bad would happen. Even today, this still affects my life. If I want to get up in the morning early and get something done that I have as a goal for my life, I feel afraid and tormented because that might mean I lose something. That might mean someone gets hurt. That might mean that God is tricking me to take something away from me.

Throughout my entire healing journey, I have had excruciating pain in my heart. This is a physical pain in my body. This pain is greatest when things are going well. As I write, I have pain in my physical heart. This pain was put as foundation programming to remind me that I have an evil heart. I have been healed layer after layer, but there are still other layers to this programming. The most recent area that Papa God has been healing has had to do with NASA. In the programming, I was put on a gravity machine for training astronauts. This machine spins on an axis. They take your hands and feet and stretch them as far as they can and then strap you into the cage. There are electrodes that are placed on your hands, heart, sexual part, and feet. There is a halo that is placed on your head to cause electric shock. As you're spinning, you are electrocuted in these areas to cause extreme pain. This is performed as a test to see how much pain you can endure before submitting to do what they ask you to do. I tried and tried to endure the pain, but it was too great. My programmers told me they were superhuman and that I could be like them. They had asked the demons to take their body and shape it into whatever they wanted. They willfully gave their entire body to be used by Satan. I can't explain the terror a person feels when they see another human being shift into another being. I can say that the movies about werewolves, vampires, and zombies are not just movies that have been made up. There are actual people who have chosen for their blood, their body, their spirit, every single bit of who they are to be changed into a demonic form. I was terrified of them, and I didn't want to be like them. They knew how terrified I was, so they hooked me up to a blood transfusion and said that the same blood that went through my veins went through their veins. They said if I did what they told me to do, I would be able to save the boys, "my brothers," from being that way. So at that point, I did the hideous things they said to do. There was no way out, no other alternative. After I was forced to do what they said, the programmers said that God had rejected me and sent me away. To make me feel like I had been sent away, I was put into the cabin that had no gravity and left there by myself. I thought I had been sent into space and would never be found. To take this even further and make them look like my rescuers, they showed up again and said that my heart had been found to be black. So they stated that I was sent to the black hole "hell" by God. According to them, the black hole was a place where the rejects and failed experiments went. If I did good enough there, competed, and won, then I could get another chance at real life. The constant hell of trying to be good enough and to save people continued nonstop. I was taken to NASA and programmed many times. This programming has taken the longest to surface because of the depth of the involvement of the government in this type of programming. They buried this programming very deep so that it would never be exposed. There are members of the Illuminati in every walk of life who try to infiltrate and pollute governments, businesses, and churches; and the list goes on.

Chapter 6

Infancy to Five Years Old

"Who will rise up for me against the wicked? Who will stand
for me against those who practice iniquity?" Psalms 94:16

Yesterday, my husband and I went to church. The pastor began to
sing old hymns the evil people used in rituals. They would play the
hymns while they did hideous things. Every aspect of church was
perverted and desecrated for me. As I was singing, the Lord said He
was restoring these hymns to me to show me what they really meant.
As I was praying, I felt a strong sense of denial. Anytime there is
strong denial, Papa God is exposing beliefs that are programming in
my mind. The programmers layered denial in continually to bury
their involvement. Only Jesus could destroy all of the layers of denial
and bring out the truth so I could be free!

I had an intense sense of grief today. When I was in slavery, I
had two other people who were supposedly my brothers. Whether
they were my biological brothers or not, I do not know for sure.
They are still in slavery. Their minds have continued to block out the
torture and pain in order to survive. Recently, my younger brother
showed up here. He is being used to try and get me to go back by
the Illuminati. The evil people sent him here to manipulate me to try
and protect him; that was my role in his life. I can remember from
the time I first saw him, I was placed in the role of his mother. If I
did not act and perform perfectly, he would not get to eat. If I didn't

do what they told me to do, he would get tortured and raped. The truth was that they tortured, starved, and raped him no matter how perfectly I behaved for them. I tried to be his savior. They did rituals just to make me take ownership of him and remind me that I was evil. The goal of them sending him was to try to access the parts that had to take care of him. The reason they sent him, just like they have many times previously, was to trigger the deepest pain I have. The pain that I was unable to rescue him was hideous. I tried with every breath in my being to rescue him, and I could not do it. When Papa God rescued me, He told me the very best way I could help him was to live in genuine freedom. As the time passes, he will see that he also can be free. My prayers are that the walls of denial are destroyed and the memories are released. I pray that he gets free from their mind control. It's a hideous feeling to know that someone that you love is being tortured, and there is nothing at all you can do about it. So I push on to be healed more and more and to expose the evil of what they do so that he can get free also. I pray and trust that Papa God will rescue my brothers like He has promised. If I was there still, neither of us would ever be free. If I went back, I would be doing the worst most selfish thing I could possibly do. It's difficult because people don't understand this; they don't see past the natural into what is under the surface. The things that I have seen. They don't know the depth of the mind control my brothers are under. The programmers used us against each other throughout our entire life. They used the love of Jesus within us against us and the fact that we are not evil like them. We were tortured the most when they made us hurt each other. The evil people know that the worst thing they can do to Papa God is to hurt His children that is the Illuminati's goal.

The programmers specifically play a movie showing what Jesus did on the cross for us early in our programming. As the movie is being played, they do a ritual to make us believe the opposite of what the Jesus film says. They torture us to believe lies about Jesus. They say that He hates us and they dress up like Jesus, then rape and torture us. The power of what Jesus did for us, even after all of the torture is still imprinted on our minds and hearts. That shows you the power of the Holy Spirit and what Honest Jesus did for us. After the rape and torture and the movie is over, the programmers tell us we can choose or not choose Jesus. I cried out to Jesus in my mind, even though they tortured me, because the Holy Spirit was working despite the torture. His love is more powerful than every single day of being tortured, tormented, and raped. Even after the specific mind control programming to convince me that Honest Jesus hates me, I knew there had to be a God that was different from what they showed me.

Along with the twisting of the truth about who Honest Jesus is, each Scripture has been twisted to make Jesus look evil. The programmers would chain me down and force me to listen to the scriptures that talked about judgment. Each verse that spoke of judgment and evil, I was told it was specifically speaking of me. "Perfect practice makes perfect" is a phrase that they would say to me over and over. I was filled with anger because no matter how hard I tried, it was never good enough. In normal situations, when you are practicing something, there is no life or death results. But in the rituals, if you didn't do something perfectly, someone died. In today's society, if someone expects perfection, it usually causes lies to form in the person about their self-worth. They may have a tendency to work for love. In my situation, the result of requiring perfection always had an end result of torture, rape, and death. The truth that I know now is that no matter how perfect I was, the same results would have happened. The programmers had no intention of stopping the torture. For example, if I made a specific phone call for them (every phone call had an agenda), if I did not speak exactly as they had trained me to speak and say exactly what they wanted me to say, the threat was that I would have to torture the person on the other side of the phone. Even if I had performed perfectly, they would torture me and say I was evil. There was no way out, no way to be free, and no way to make my own choices.

Every time I would take a call in private, they would send a shock to my ear. If I did not say what they wanted me to say, then they would shock me. No matter how much I tried, I could never say exactly what they wanted me to say. There was always something I got wrong, even if I said exactly what they told me to say. The phone call was scored, and my entire day was scored. If the score was low, someone, including myself, got hurt. After getting free, I have worked for a customer service company that scored my performance on every detail of my phone call. It brought back memories; and I would feel intense fear, that no matter what I said, I did something wrong or I could have done better. During most of the customer-service types of jobs, I feel like I'm going to a ritual every single day. Even though the reality is that I'm not being tortured, the feelings are just as intense as if I was still being tortured. On the phone, I feel the same way when I was getting tortured and graded for each call in the rituals. Even though there is no torture now and there is just occasional verbal abuse on the phone by people who are upset about their issues, the feelings still feel like the hell I was in, just without torture. This is how my life is still being affected even today by the hell that the programmers put me through. Torture, rape, and abuse not only affect you then; they affect you for the rest of your life. These feelings continue until Papa God heals those lies and wounds. Then you can move on in freedom. Since the torture I went through was all day every day for thirty years, it is an ongoing journey of healing throughout each day. But there is not anything too big for Papa God! He is untangling the lies of the evil people one day at a time and bringing truth!

This book is dedicated and written for every person who is in slavery, for every person who is being controlled, and for every person who believes there is no way out. There is a way out, and Papa God is the way out! He will move heaven and earth to rescue you! There is truly no pit too deep that Papa God can't pull you from. This is also written for every person who is called by Papa God to set the captive free, and that is all of us! He has called us to be a light in the darkness. "Let your light so shine before men, that they may see your good works and glorify your Father in heaven" (Matthew 5:16). This may seem like a task that is impossible in the current pain you're enduring. Or there maybe people you feel are just too broken and wounded that they couldn't possibly be healed and shine for Jesus. I can testify that there is a Papa God that is big enough and wise enough that He can bring healing to all wounds caused by the enemy—and cause us to shine, as we were created to shine!

Papa God has called us to set the captive free. "The Spirit of the Lord is upon Me, Because He has anointed Me. To preach the gospel to the poor; He has sent Me to heal the brokenhearted, to proclaim liberty to the captives and recovery of sight to the blind, to set at liberty those who are oppressed" (Luke 4:18). There is something you can do! You can set the captive free. You have the power of Papa God within you. This will be a challenging task but will be worth every second. At the end, you will have no doubts that you helped give someone freedom, and their life will never be the same! Isn't that worth being uncomfortable? The Holy Spirit in you is saying, "Yes, it's worth it!"

Evil in this culture can sometimes be difficult to recognize. It hides in normal things, like people you think you know. Unfortunately, recognizing evil isn't the hardest part. It's the task of standing up to evil even though nobody else will; that is the hardest. We are living beneath a dam that's holding years and years of evil. You can say that that dam is not going to break all you want; but when the rains come and that dam bursts, all that bad comes out. You won't have time to run for high ground! Now is the time! Now is the time to arm yourself with truth. Now is the time to get the strategies of heaven and knowledge of the enemy's plots and schemes! First Peter 5:8 says, "Stay alert! Watch out for your enemy, the devil. He prowls around like a roaring lion, looking for someone to devour."

As I write, there is a dove that landed on my balcony, and I feel like it is looking directly at me. I feel like it is a beautiful reminder of peace from heaven, that Papa God's got this! He will rescue the captive, and He will raise up people to fight for freedom for those who don't have the strength to fight. It will not be an easy battle, but it will be worth every second. So what do you say? Are you willing to take this journey? He will be beside you every step of the way.

I'm now going to unfold my story in a detailed chronological order, a step at a time, to make sure that no detail is missed. I want each person to grasp the magnitude and depth of the Illuminati's and satanic cults' hold over our society and over thousands of innocent people. There are people out there who need someone to believe them. They need people to believe that they experienced this torture too. There are people out there who have been called "crazy" for sharing the truth of their experience. Unfortunately, a lot of the people who are in disbelief are from the church. The church, the very place we should be welcomed and accepted no matter what. The "unknown" causes fear in people. Fear causes people to shrink away and find ways to dismiss things that are uncomfortable. Scientifically, it is proven that the brain continually tries to stay in homeostasis. Our brain enters into homeostasis; it tries to stay stable, on an equilibrium. So even our brain tries to push away a truth that is too big for us to understand or fathom, it takes a deliberate choice to acknowledge and see the truth. I can guarantee you that there is an evil much bigger than what we can imagine, but that does not diminish the greatness of God. The acknowledgment of the fact that there is great evil in this world only gives us the ability and knowledge to stand against it and fight it strategically. If you go into war, don't you want a plan? God always gave His people a plan when they went into war, even if the plan didn't make sense to them. How can you fight what you're not even aware of? My goal is to make you aware so you will be prepared for the battle.

During the process of writing this book, the sadness was overwhelming at times. I have dealt with the pain of my conception with the Lord, but, obviously, there was another layer that needed to be surfaced. The truth that I know now after a decade of healing is that Papa God formed me, and He knew me before I was born. The reality of what happened is that I was put in a petri dish and mixed with all the Illuminati bloodlines. The DNA of the people who were my programmers were also mixed in so that I would look like them. I will go into much more detail about programmers in this book so you will be aware of what and who they are. A very basic description of the programmer is the person who is a member of the Illuminati or cult who continually tortures, abuses, and rapes a person to control what they think and do. Their goal is to make the person do and think exactly what they want them to.

The Illuminati believe that there is only one chosen race—a pure race that is perfect. They believe all other races need to be exterminated. People with handicaps, the elderly, the Jews, the Christians, anybody who is not in the Illuminati bloodline should be done away with. The Illuminati DNA is linked to every mountain of influence in this culture. For example, in media and entertainment, there are Illuminati at the top of these mountains. Specifically, this is done so that what people watch and what people hear is what the Illuminati chooses for people to watch and hear. Therefore, all of people's thoughts and actions are controlled by what the Illuminati wants.

At the root of my conception, I was designated a "mixed breed." As a "mixed breed," I was to carry on the chosen Illuminati races. I had to take the role of "Mary" and breed with whom the programmers said to breed with. The people I bred with were my chosen "Jesus." This was done to create the perfect generational line, according to my programmers. In the programming, we were told that the real Jesus rejected us because we were a mixed breed. We did not carry the perfect unified bloodline. So the real Jesus would only accept us if we could achieve perfection. They would recite in the ritual, "Be perfect as I am perfect" (Matthew 5:48). This is the scripture that the programmers used to substantiate that they were perfect and I was not. The mixed breeds were not perfect, and were not chosen for salvation.

The programmers inserted me from the petri dish into a lady they called my mother. I had very specific memories of this happening. Papa God surfaced these memories to give me insight to all that I went through. The memories about my DNA were the most difficult memories to handle. They took the longest for Papa God to bring to the surface. I believe that, partly, this had to do with the fact that every human being wants to belong. Belonging and acceptance is a basic human need. The lady who carried me in her womb was a victim. Papa God has shown me since then that He considers her my real mom. She had pure love for me, and she was Papa God's child. Spiritual family is much stronger than biological family. This is because, as Christians, we live by the spirit! I will meet my mom someday in heaven. I got a vision from the Lord of my mom in heaven. This vision from Papa God brought great healing; that's how I know it was from Papa God. I'm still healing from the lies about my mixed-breed bloodline. Papa God has shown me that I have His blood in my veins, and ultimately all blood is from Papa God. This has had power over my thinking because of their programming. I was programmed to think blood is the only thing that matters.

As I was in the womb, the programmers would chant over and over that I was the seed of Satan. They inserted the EVOL machine (electrocution) into the lady's womb that carried me. This was a device that they used over and over again throughout my life to use shock to torture me. So while I was in her womb, I was experiencing electric shock. Also, when I was in the womb, they inserted a vibrator to stimulate my genitals and played music of a heartbeat at the same time. This was to program me that sex was the only way I would be alive and stay alive. They wanted me to bond to sex. They said over and over that sex was the only reason God would allow me to be born. As I was being born, the programmers pushed me back into the womb over and over again. They said I had to work harder to get out. They spoke over me that no one wanted me, not even God. This caused rage and anger toward myself that I could not do what they were telling me to do. Also, they wanted to break my spirit so that I would not fight against them and give up.

It's difficult for people to believe that I can remember these things that happened before I was even born, and I understand that. As I have been on this healing journey, Papa God has brought me back to those places. I would literally sound like a crying infant when I would be reliving the flashbacks, with all of the same emotions that a baby would have. This remembering and allowing Papa God to speak to me brought great healing to my life, so that is my proof that it is real. As my mom carried me in her womb, I bonded with her. She was an innocent victim, a "breeder." The breeder was someone who was chosen to carry children in their womb, and breed with whomever they told them to. When they are done with the breeding, the breeders are killed. She was a victim. She was also tortured to breed and carry babies that were put inside of her, whether they were conceived by her or inserted into her. Even as a baby in a mother's womb, I felt her love. I would never feel love again from a human being until I was almost thirty years old. According to scientific studies, during their time in the womb, babies hear, feel, and even smell their mothers. ("How Your Baby Learns to Love" by Sheryl Berk from *American Baby*.)

While I was in the womb, the programmers put a clamp on my head and pulled me out of the womb. They said that the clamp was my crown and that I was evil because I wanted the crown. They did this to cause me to believe that I was evil at the core of my being. Then when I was born, they killed my mom. The programmers spoke over and over that her death was my fault. They chanted that I was so evil I made my mom die. Anytime they chanted words over people, they played music that took the person into another spiritual realm and another conscious state. This made the words go deep into the unconscious realm where they were buried. The evil the programmers do are specifically hidden in the unconscious mind.

The programmers then wrapped the umbilical cord around my neck until I turned blue. They put me on the operating table and took a knife and slit my mom's belly. They spoke out torture levels to my mind. Then the music and chanting activated a serpent spirit to enter me. They said that I strangled my mom and that God was strangling me with her umbilical cord because I was so evil. The programmer said my heart killed my mom. At the same time, they stimulated my genitals. They said they gave me the sex feelings, because that was the only way Jesus would save me. All of this made me believe even as an infant that I was so evil that God wanted to get rid of me. Also, the programmers wanted me to believe the lie that I was so evil I caused everybody I cared about to die. At that point, the programmers put me in a body bag with my mom and told me if I was good enough I could bring her back. Of course, I couldn't bring her back, but as an infant, I didn't know that. So I learned to hate myself and see myself as completely evil. The next phase in the torture was to get me to bond with my programmers and to think that in order for me to survive I needed them to torture me.

I remember being in a little glass cage as an infant. I was connected to a monitor that showed me if my heart was beating or not.

The rest of my body was covered with electrodes; wires were going everywhere. The evil people said they were keeping me alive. When they showed me that my heart was beating, they locked the cage. When they showed me that my heart wasn't beating, they unlocked the cage. As an infant, I didn't know what they were doing, but as they continued to do things, I learned that they controlled my every move.

"We determine if you live or die," they said over and over to me. If I moved, I was electrocuted. They trained my mind through torture. In every move I made on my own, they shocked me. I learned to stay still and only move when I was told to move. When I would cry, I would be electrocuted, so I learned not to cry. I was then told over and over that I wasn't really hurting, because I wasn't crying. "You're not even hurting. You are not crying!" They said over and over I was faking the pain. So there was a constant state of confusion.

The programmers made me intentionally bond with people. Then they would rip the person away from me or kill them. I would be put in isolation, completely alone, for long periods of time. The reason the programmers did this was to get my mind to bond to them, and no one else. They said they were doing me a favor. They said they would never leave me because I needed to be tortured. Even though they tortured me, I thought that having somebody control me was the only way I would stop hurting people. My mind bonded to the evil people because they were there, even if it was to torture and rape me. This caused a division in my mind due to the torture of human deprivation. The worst torture is complete isolation and seclusion. This causes a human being to have such a human deficit and feelings of rejection that they will do anything to have people with them, even if the people cause hideous pain.

The programmers intentionally created a part of my mind they called the *master executioner*. This part was created during the torture that was done in the underground military compounds used for Monarch MK Ultra Programming. The agenda for this programming is to create soldiers for the end-time agenda of the Illuminati.

There are tunnels underground, built specifically for travel and torture, within all large cities. The victims are forced to watch while people are skinned alive. The victims are told that the people who are skinned were not obedient. They have to stay a caterpillar because they didn't do their job as a soldier. Their skins would be hanging upside down all over the room to remind the other victims that they stayed a caterpillar instead of becoming a butterfly.

Chapter 7

Details to Expose

"Have nothing to do with the fruitless deeds of darkness,
but rather expose them." Ephesians 5:11-12

Hitler and Mengele were demonically connected to each of the victims. The reason the Illuminati does this is they want to cause as much demonic bondage as they can to the victims. The stronger the generational demonic hold is, the better, the easier it is for the Illuminati to enslave people.

> Dr. Josef Mengele, nicknamed the Angel of Death, and the other Nazi doctors at the death camps tortured men, women, and children and did medical experiments of unspeakable horror during the Holocaust. Victims were put into pressure chambers, tested with drugs, castrated, frozen to death. Children were exposed to experimental surgeries performed without anesthesia, transfusions of blood from one to another, isolation endurance, reaction to various stimuli. The doctors made injections with lethal germs, sex change operations, removal of organs and limbs. At Auschwitz Josef Mengele did a number of medical experiments, using twins. These twins as

young as five years of age were usually murdered after the experiment was over and their bodies dissected. Mengele injected chemicals into the eyes of the children in an attempt to change their eye color. He carried out twin-to-twin transfusions, stitched twins together, castrated or sterilized twins. Many twins had limbs and organs removed in macabre surgical procedures, performed without using an anesthetic. (Louis Bulow, the Holocaust.)

The type of experiments and torture I went through were based partly on Mengele's experiments on torture and the mind.

The Illuminati labels the victims number 1 or number 2. The number 2s were the dogs, and the number 1s were gods. I was called a number 2. The number 2s were put alone in a room, and all of the people in the ritual would use the bathroom on them. The feces were smeared all over us. We were left for weeks in a room by ourselves with the feces still on us. The gods were told that they could cause the parts of their physical body to be able to be joined together and have power. In this ritual, they would torture us by forcing our hands to cut a baby into five parts using a knife. We were told that the different body parts could be put back together and the baby could go to heaven if we chose to be god. As the god part, if we saved the baby that was cut up, there would be a savior for the mixed breeds. In order to have the savior, we were forced to be god, the judge at the end. This was a hideous position. They made us think that, as gods, we were in control of who would live or die. The worst possible feeling was to have to decide who lived or died.

During the first five years of my life, I was in a hospital-like setting. My surroundings were sterile white, and people were dressed in all white. There was no furniture in the rooms, just machines for torture. There were many empty white rooms with other infants like me in cages. The programmers said that I was in heaven and that god had put me there. I was programmed to believe that, since I wasn't the chosen race, I was put there to torture continuously, to make me perfect. I could not see anyone's face, because they had surgical masks on. They would electrocute the right side of my body until I was numb and poke me with needles. At the same time, the programmers showed me normal pictures of themselves, and they said they were perfect. They put a black cover over the left side of my body and said the left side was evil. To make me believe I was evil, they shaved the left side of my head. They put skin irritants on my body to cause whelps all over the left side of my body. They chanted over an over that the left side was evil. I literally thought I was two different people. The Mengele twin programming. The programmers would tell the left side of my body to hold the pain. Then they covered the right side of my body with a pink blanket and forced my left hand to stab people with a knife. The middle part of my mind and body was called the "flat line." This was the sex part that they trained to have sex. They fed me sugar or injected me with sugar in the right side to cause disassociation. The evil people said the "flat line" was where the Illuminati and seed of Satan was planted. They would hold my left eye open and shine light in that eye. This was to cause the brain to store information where they wanted it to. There was an oath they forced me to take as the Illuminati queen. I was forced to swear to stay on the right side and not see any of the evil that was being done to me. The programmers said I could rule instead of being tortured if I chose to forget. If I chose to forget the truth, then I would be allowed to get clothes and food. The torture and programming was done to get my mind in a war within itself. Each part of my brain was deliberately programmed to hate the other. This further insured the evil people that the truth would not surface, because of the torture to the brain. My brain would not allow the truth to surface. The programmers were experts at how the brain functioned. They forced a right-and-left-brain disconnect on purpose.

The programmers used sex and sugar to numb my emotions. They used addiction to control me, whether it was sugar, sex, drugs, or whatever they chose to get me addicted to. Sex and sugar was used in experiments with me, much like the Pavlov studies. When sugar or sex was given to me, they would kill someone at the same time. So every time I got sugar or sex, I immediately felt guilty and fearful because I knew someone was going to get killed or hurt. This produced hatred toward myself because I was feeling good feelings from the addictive substances as someone was being killed. When the programmers took sugar and sex away, they would put me in a room alone with dead bodies and body parts. They said that I had killed and cut up the people in the room because I didn't have sex and sugar. So even though I was afraid of someone dying when I had the sugar and sex, I was much more terrified of not having sex and sugar, because I thought I would be left alone to be out of control and kill people. Sugar was also used over and over because of the influence on the brain. It is eight times more addictive than cocaine. As well, it's an acceptable drug in our culture. Sugar is killing and controlling us, but unfortunately people don't know the true reason it was introduced into society. It was introduced specifically to control people and get them sick. This was a very strategic plan of the Illuminati, and they are very prideful that they got away with it. Their goal was to bring something into our culture that would make people sick and control them, and that which no one would question. I will go into that in more detail later.

Throughout my infancy and as a toddler, I lived in deprivation. As an infant, they gave me semen in a bottle. They said semen was all I deserved because I was a whore. They said over and over that I was born for sex, and that sex was the only gift God gave me. They tortured me to believe God gave people sex but He condemned every person who had sex outside of marriage. Then He laughed at me because He knew I wasn't good enough to be married. According to the programmers, it was a trick planned out by God. The programmers told me that God really gave me no gifts and condemned me completely. I was told from the beginning He only put up with me. The programmers made me think that God said I was a whore and that sex was the only thing that controlled me from being a killer, so He paid them to rape me and sell me. Of course, they took pictures of me as an infant sucking on a penis. And other sexual photos that were positioned as though I had chosen to have sex. They said the pictures proved I was a whore.

The spiritual and bloodline ties are established at infancy intentionally. This is done so that the Illuminati has a foundation for all of the programming. The spiritual and bloodline ties are formed in many ways. The computer is used to cause a foundation of demonic roots. There is a computer that is powered on during rituals, and different electronic sensors are placed on the victim and the computer. This is to cause a magnetic and electronic frequency between the person and the computer, which the demons can be channeled through. They also scan the eye with an electronic sensor since the eye is the window to the soul. The programmers then assign a number to each victim, a computer programming number. Then they do a ritual where there is blood spilled and put on each part of the body where the computer sensors are. They call in the demons and territorial spirits to travel through the sensors and into other dimensions to cause a soul tie with the territorial spirits over regions of the world. The leaders of that region astral project and summon demons to cause an overlay or demonic force field around victims. This is what demonically keeps ministers or counselors from getting through to the core person or the hard drive when doing ministry with Illuminati victims.

The computer and the person are joined demonically. This allows people to remotely access victims through chips placed in the body through electrical frequencies. The Illuminati want everything about who they are and what they do to be so hidden that no one would have physical proof of what has been done. The frequencies are a way that they get away with their schemes in most of the communication they have with other world powers. If they meet and communicate on a different radio wave frequency that people are not aware of, then the purposes and plans that they have for this country cannot be exposed.

Another way the programmers establish a demonic foundation is through grid systems. The Illuminati plot each move that they are going to make on a grid system, physically and spiritually. The reason they do this is so they know where the portals are, for example, where high corporate rituals are done. Then they demonically connect the primary hubs and portals to each town and city and state. The victims are assigned to different grids physically and spiritually, and they are given assignments based on the grid system. There are concentration camps and corporate ritual sites set up for their end-time agenda based on where the demonic portals and territorial powers are set up. The victims are linked like a chain, and if any victim gets free, that causes a loss of power because it weakens the grid system.

The programmers and the Illuminati put cameras everywhere. They told me that they taped everything all the time. When I was put to sleep, by giving me drugs, the programmers would set up a situation where a person would be killing somebody, and they would take a video of them from the back. The person would have the same kind of hair as mine and the same clothes on; then they would say, "That was you killing people." I believed that if they didn't torture me, I would always be killing and hurting people. I was told over and over that if I wasn't being tortured, my real heart would be exposed, the heart that was caught on camera doing the evil things. To me, the worst hell was not knowing what I had done and waking up after they had given me the drugs. The programmers told me over and over that I lived in a camera. So I had intense confusion. I thought every single thing about me wasn't real, that I was an actress all the time. The programmers set me up time after time. They tried to force my mind to believe that I wasn't capable of knowing what was real and what wasn't, so I had to rely on them (programmers) to tell me what was real. They buried me and a baby with a camera and then covered us with dirt. I was forced to say out loud, "I take the demons so the baby can live." The baby stopped crying, and I kept taking the demons to try and get her to live. Their goal was to trick me to allow the demons in. The baby never came back to life. She didn't survive.

The depth of denial and programming of the Illuminati is shown clearly in the movie *The Truman Show*. The man in the movie had been living a life controlled by everybody around him. They were filming him all the time. He was the only person (denial part) who wasn't aware that his life wasn't real. In the movie, the people were inside a control room deciding what he saw and what he did every day. This is an actual ritual; that is what the evil people do to victims. It is not a movie; it is reality for millions of people in this world. The movie was just a way to desensitize people to the truth. The producer in the movie Christof is a good depiction of a real-life programmer that is molding his experiment (victim) to be exactly who he says to be.

So many movies today are based on actual rituals. There are more evil movies than there are good ones. The entertainment industry is controlled by the Illuminati. This is a way to keep victims updated on their programming. What I mean by that is when they see the movie, it reinforces their programming. Another reason for the infiltration of the entertainment industry is to cause people to be desensitized from seeing the truth. When people see a movie that is based on a ritual and then a victim shares their story, people are more prone to say that the victim got their memories from a movie. The reality and the truth is the movie was copied from the ritual. An example of a movie that people think is very pure and that is filled with programming is the current movie *Wonder Woman*. Wonder Woman is named Diana. Diana is a "god." She is a Greek god of hunting and childbirth. The Greek gods are used in Illuminati programming. They named a part of my mind Diana. The reason they did this was to force me to believe that I hunted people to kill them. The Diana part was forced to kill and have sex with many people. They programmed that part to think she wanted the sex and the killing. I was forced to be an aggressor in sex, or they would kill people. The programmers take the different regions of the universe and the Greek gods they are associated with; then they claim that area with a demonic throne. There is a ritual with a human sacrifice that is done to create a portal and power source for the demons.

Chapter 8

Triggers

"Woe to those who call evil good and good evil, who put darkness for light and light for darkness, who put bitter for sweet and sweet for bitter." Isaiah 5:20

Foundational triggers are programmed into the victim at zero to five years of age. The reason they program in triggers is so that when the victim hears a noise, sees a picture, hears a song, or looks at a picture, and thousands of other triggers; it reinforces their control over the mind. For example, the programmers tied me up and let water drip on my forehead over and over again; at the same time, they would stimulate my genitals. This caused me to have sexual feelings every time I heard the water drip. The same out-of-control crazy feeling that happened when they tortured me would start again when I heard the sound of water dripping. Another example is the ticking of a clock. I was put in a room with only a clock that ticked loudly. Then my genitals were stimulated on purpose so that when I heard the clock, I would have sexual feelings. This created an out-of-control feeling; that was the Illuminati's goal, because then I would need them to control me. Other examples are chewing gum, tapping your foot, clearing your throat, coughing, sneezing, and sniffling just to name a few. The programmers chose these things because they would happen every day all day.

The programmers used phrases and words to be trigger words. The word *come* was said over and over. At the same time, they would use equipment that stimulated my genitals. This torture was done so that in normal conversation when a person said *come* in a sentence, I would automatically have sexual feelings. I would immediately feel shame and fear. The word *know* was also used as a trigger word. Since *know* is in the Bible as a sexual encounter, they would read the Bible and stimulate my genitals. Every time I heard the word *know* in daily life, I thought it meant sex. When people read the Bible, I would have sexual feelings because my body had been trained to respond to those words. My thoughts were, *I must surely be disgusting and need someone to control me if I have sexual feelings while someone is reading the Bible.* They told me over and over that I was sick and that I thought about sex all the time. Since *know* was used as a sexual reference in the Bible, it was also very confusing. The programmers would dress up like Jesus and rape me, to get to "know" me. I never wanted anybody to "know" me. This made me shut down any feelings I had, because I was afraid to feel.

Another goal of the programmers, as we discussed, was to get me so terrified of myself that I believed that I needed the torture and control. When I was in the hospital, they starved me, poked my eyes with needles to make them look red, and shaved my head. They wanted me to look like a demon. They told me I was a demon, and they called me a demon. My name at that time sounded like the word *demon*. So they said, "We gave you that name, because we know who you really are." Then they would put me in front of a mirror and say, "This is who you really are." I looked like a demon; therefore, I was a demon.

There were many other infants and children there in the hospital setting where I was put. The programmers intentionally tried to turn all of us victims against each other so we wouldn't trust or bond with each other. They knew that there is power in numbers, and if we bonded together, we would be stronger. I was separated from all the others with a glass wall in between us. The only time they allowed us to be together was when they were torturing us. When it was time for the rituals, the programmers would bring the other infants and children food, clothing, blankets, and basic needs. Then they would bring in people to pick them up, like they were taking them out of the hospital. As I saw this happening, they would say, "Those children are the chosen race, and you are not." "If you become perfect, we will give you what you need." They told me to be perfect meant to have sex, breed, kill, pretend, and anything else they said to do to be "perfect." The truth has been revealed through my healing, as Papa God has shown me, that the other children never got anything either. The programmers set up that situation to trick each of us. The reality, Papa God revealed to me is that the evil people took back everything from the victims or paired the good things with sex and killing so that there would be intense guilt. No child or infant ever got anything good there; even basic needs were not met in that hideous hospital.

As I said earlier, I was told that I was the race that they called the "mixed breed" or dog. The programmers put a dog leash on me and walked me around like a dog. They forced me to complete commands like sit, stand, speak, and lay down. The word *god* is *dog* backward. The programmers said I was the exact opposite of god because of my DNA, so I was a dog. They would put a bowl of dog food in front of me and make me eat like a dog. I was forced to growl at anybody that tried to take away my dog food. This is another programmed way they pit victims against each other. The programmers would sometimes put only one dog food bowl in front of us, and everybody had to try and eat. This created division and competition between all of us in order to get even our basic needs met. There were programs to get us to have confusion and guilt over our survival instinct. If we ate, then that meant that some other person didn't eat and might die. This torture was used as a foundation to be able to control what we would eat daily, so we would be thin and easier to sell. Along with getting us deliberately addicted to sugar, they were creating a "damned if you do, damned if you don't" situation. Their goal was to create intense guilt when eating so they could keep us thin. They wanted to be able to control our weight at all times.

Drugs were another way that the programmers controlled me. They forced different drug needles into my arms and made me get addicted. The drugs would make me foggy and disoriented. The programmers said that if I took the drugs I would forget the evil that was going on. After they got me addicted, they would take away the drugs. This would cause hideous withdrawal symptoms. They wanted me to get to a place that I would do whatever they asked me to do, because of the intense pain of the withdrawal from the drugs. As a child, drug withdrawals are brutal and traumatizing to say the least.

The programmers core lie was that I was born evil. They said if I didn't pretend they were good and have sex, they would put me back in the hole. This was a hole beside the house they lived in; they called it Satan's womb. It meant utter darkness forever. Coke was also used in denial programming, consistently. I was given Coca-Cola (Coke) from birth, and it contained cocaine and many other addictive ingredients. In the rituals, the Illuminati members stand in a circle and put the Coke bottle in the middle and chant repeatedly: *Cum Over Killing Every day, Cum Over Killing Everybody*, an acrostic for the word *coke*. Then Coke is given to the victim to drink. The victim is told the Coke makes them want to have sex. Then the victim is raped. After that, they ejaculate on the victim. The Illuminati chant over the victim and call in demonic powers to "burn the evil out of the victim." So on a daily basis, I thought that if I drank the Coke, the evil within me would not be seen. To reinforce this thinking, the programmers kill someone in the ritual circle. Then they pour the Coke on the dead person and the victim. The Coke takes off the blood, so they believe that the Coke will remove the evil. There is an addictive demonic force at the root of the Coke industry. This exists on purpose to kill and control Americans without them being aware of what is happening.

The programmers would set food in front of me, but I wouldn't be allowed to eat any of the food. They would allow other people to eat while I was watching. The programmers said the people were allowed to eat because the other people were good and I was not good. I was tortured to hate fat intensely and hate myself if I had any fat on me. No matter how big I was, they told me that I was fat. If they said that I was fat, I wasn't allowed to eat until they said so.

While in the hospital, the programmers put me in a room that they called "hell." There were body parts and dismembered people in the room. They said I had killed and dismembered the people. They made me stay alone in hell with the body parts. This was excruciatingly painful. They told me that this was hell because I had to eternally live with the fact that I was a killer. I felt terror when I thought that I didn't have anybody to control me. The worst part was that I couldn't remember doing any of what they said I did. So I thought I was crazy. Exactly what the programmers wanted. I was terrified to not get tortured by them. In my mind, the torture and control was what kept people safe from me and how evil I was. For example, they had a fish in a fish tank, and they said it was fine before I was in the room. They left the room, and they said the fish died because I came in there and killed it. I said, "I don't remember doing that." They said I did remember and that I was lying. I constantly thought I was doing evil and I just didn't remember it.

There were rooms in the hospital that they used for gas chambers. They would take children into the rooms and tell me the only way the children could get to heaven is if I turn the gas on. The alternative for the children they presented was hell. Hell meant I would have to kill them and dismember them. I had been tortured to believe, as I shared before, that I killed and dismembered people in hell. I had no other choice. Constantly, they put me in a double bind. Everything they said was a "choice" was bad. I was always trying to find the least evil choice. Reality is that I never had a choice. I never got to choose anything. After thinking I had saved the children, the programmers showed me the children were dead. I was tormented and full of excruciating sadness. The programmers would then say, "Why did you do that? You're evil. We didn't tell you to do that!"

Some of the programming resembled the Nazi concentration camps. There were rituals where someone was dressed as Hitler, and he was telling all of us what to do. I had to stand in a military uniform as a child and say, "Heil Hitler." I had to pledge allegiance to Hitler and Mengele, and the mission they had for us to do in the world. The Illuminati's goal is to exterminate every person not like them. Their plan is to place the victims as soldiers in each city, in each region, and in each state. Then program us to do what that want us to do in that specific area. Therefore, they have super soldiers hidden within the US. They are trained to be ready, to be in place when the Illuminati decides to put people in concentration camps, which have already been set up. Their prideful view is that if every area is controlled by them without anybody being aware of it, then they can succeed in taking over the world. For example, global warming is an issue being pushed by actors and congressmen. The Illuminati want to eventually say that we need to get rid of the other races because they are draining our environment and natural resources. But the people in control of the money continue to be the producers of the things that are killing our environment. This is another part of their agenda.

The Illuminati brought many infants into this country to be trained as German soldiers. They are planted into this society to accomplish a mission to take down America. The last time that was attempted was when Hitler tried to get rid of the Jews. On November 3, 1943, some forty-three thousand Jews were gathered, shot, and killed from various camps in Poland. This concluded Operation *Reinhard*, which had virtually exterminated Polish Jewry. The SS called this final action "Harvest Festival." While countless historians, commentators, and books have often emphasized the industrial nature of the Holocaust, SS Nazis understood the concluding action of Operation *Reinhard* to be a special day on the farm comparable to an annual harvest celebration. In the twisted Nazi mind, Jewish weeds had to be eradicated from the blood and soil of Germany's *lebensraum*. Operation "Harvest Festival" was the single largest Nazi Jewish massacre conducted throughout the entire war. That is exactly what they were planning for Christians.

I have explained previously how they created a foundation of hatred toward myself and how that bonded me to them. The terror and hatred of myself was specifically caused to keep me with them. I believed in every fiber of my being that I was killing and raping people if I wasn't being tortured. The programmers, at the same time, were creating a foundation of denial. Every time they raped or tortured me or made me think I was evil, they said the only way out was for me to see them as a perfect family. They would hold up a picture of themselves and say, "We are perfect. If you always say we are perfect, then all of what you did will go away." I was tortured to push all of the pain, terror, and guilt down by pretending the programmers were good. For example, when they forced me to look at a picture of Jesus, they would say over and over "prey" for us, not *pray* for us. This meant if I didn't kill somebody for them, then their sins would be held against them. They said that my sins would kill them, and I had to make up for that by killing somebody to take their place. Literally as a sacrifice for my sins, since we were tortured to believe Jesus didn't die for us. Then they put a picture of themselves up on the wall for me to continually look at. If I looked at the picture of them and said they were perfect, my mind could numb out and not feel the hideous pain of having to kill someone. The truth is I didn't want to kill anybody, and I did everything to keep from having to do that! But according to them, I had to honor my father and mother (that's what they called themselves) and do what they said to do. To not honor them as parents meant a worse evil, and they used the scripture of honoring your father and mother to reinforce that lie. So now when I look at a picture of Jesus, I start to see a picture of the programmers and see them as perfect. When I look behind that denial picture and genuinely feel the pain of what was done, I see the killing that I was forced to do to honor them. That truth wrenches my being because I never had a choice.

The evil people tortured me deliberately to create as many parts of my mind as possible. The reason they do this is to get a specific part of my mind to do a job or function. Also, if the programmers divided my mind purposely, then the truth was buried deeper, and they wouldn't be found out. For example, there was a Pain part that carried the pain. This part was told that they created me to be in pain and that I was born to be in pain. There was a part they named Demon. I was forced to make sounds like a demon and look like a demon. If I did what they said, I would be able to keep people from dying, and when I got older, I could keep my child from dying. The programmers said they were keeping me from hurting people, and even from hurting my children. There was a part they named

Stupid. They often used acrostics, STUPID meant, Satan Trained Under Person in Denial. The evil people made me act stupid, and they said if I didn't act stupid, they would tell everybody that I was evil. The stupid part had to deny the truth continually and pretend everything was perfect. There was a part they named the Breeder. There were generational, bloodline, and DNA rites to this part. The reason they said that they had to create many parts was I was evil at the core. There were millions of different parts of my mind created deliberately by the evil people.

The evil people twisted the meaning of the weapons of warfare in the Bible. They called the sword of the spirit, the penis. When I was raped, I was told it was the sword of the spirit trying to make me good. The evil people used electric shock at the same time. They trained me that the shock was always their way to get the evil out of me. They told me that evil resided in my belly and my heart. I was hooked up to an ultrasound machine, and they put an image on the screen that looked like a monster. So I thought I was an evil monster. Another way they caused fracturing of my mind into different parts was a military type of torture. They would strap me down and let a drip of water drip over and over onto my forehead. This caused anger and my mind to split off. It's a military tactic. There were thousands of denial parts. When I reference denial parts of my mind, I'm talking about parts of my mind that were forced to block every memory and every feeling of the torture and rape. "Fake it till you make it" is a well-known phrase in our culture that tries to make stuffing emotions something that is a good thing, but it is not! It causes destruction to your mind, body, and spirit. The worst result of faking is that it keeps us from having connection with people and Papa God!

I was continually forced to focus on the fake pictures of a perfect family, and I was told if I didn't focus on their perfection, I would have to see the truth of the evil I had been forced to do. This created a great division in my mind. The reality of the hideous memories of the hell I endured were under the pictures of us posing like we were a normal family. There were seed of Satan parts, pretty pink princess parts, Shirley Temple parts, just to name a few. Shirley Temple was said to be an Illuminati-trained child. She was tortured to sing and dance to the degree that she did on TV. They used Shirley Temple movies during the rituals to get me to focus on trying to be perfect. The programmers made me drink Shirley Temples, a drink that they said made me forget. The evil people made an intentional division in my mind between the denial parts and evil parts. They backed this up with specific brain torture to intentionally divide the left and the right brain. Their goal was to make the parts hate each other.

Another major denial program was sugar programming. In the ritual, I would be placed on a food pyramid, a demonic triangle. The leaders would call in principalities from all over the world to cover me with a sugar fog (coma). The sugar was supposed to cover my sins. I would then be forced to eat large amounts of sugar, and they injected sugar into my veins. The foundation of the food pyramid is essentially sugar, carbohydrates that turn into sugar. The Food and Drug Administration are controlled and have a foundation of Illuminati control. As victims, we were forced to chant, "Sugar controls us." At the same time, we had to make a vow and covenant to the Illuminati to stay in coma. This, in turn, would give the programmers more demonic control, and a denial sugar coma would be put on us. The sugar coma was induced to get us to never remember the things that they did to us.

Sugar is everywhere in our culture. Every celebration and social activity includes food. When you look at the different celebrations such as birthdays and weddings in the United States, cake is always present. Ball games have hotdogs, chicken wings, and beer. This could go on and on. It does not mean food is evil or an indulgence is evil. It does mean that we should be cautious and protective of our bodies and minds. There is an enemy who wants to destroy us, and there are people who follow that enemy that want to destroy us. The sugar program was a foundational program, because every time a victim would see people eating sugar we thought they were involved with the torture. If you talk to someone who has changed their eating habits and cut out sugar and processed food, there is a mental clarity that is regained with that choice, so the reality is that we are being drugged as a culture in general.

Along with the sugar programming, the programmers said that God created the heavens, earth, and humans in seven days. On the eighth day, the Illuminati created the "perfect" genes, the genes that God didn't want to create. This included myself since I was put together in a petri dish, the foods we (the genetically modified) were supposed to eat, and genetically modified animals. The evil people said that God didn't care about us, so He didn't create us. Also, the programmers said that God didn't give us food. This is where genetically modified food started, and cloning as well. The Illuminati is creating their own new world order. They want people to be sick. They want people to be tired and die before their time. This is why they have changed all of the food into GMO food. Food that has been processed with chemicals that they have created, that kill us. Plant-based food is from Papa God, and studies show consistently that plant-based foods heal our bodies. But the people who control the food and drug industry have gotten us addicted to sugar and processed foods, and our everyday experience is connected to those genetically modified foods. These foods cause cancer and every other type of disease in the body. The culture has bought the lies, and these genetically modified foods are killing us.

Another way the Illuminati is trying to take over the world is by getting people into a different state of consciousness. When evil people can get the minds of people into a passive state of consciousness, then they have more power over their thinking and actions. This is their biggest weapon of war, because people are unaware of what things are causing their mind to go into a submissive trance-like state. I'm aware of this because of the torture and rituals that I endured. The programmers would hypnotize me by making me breathe a certain way for me to go into an altered state of consciousness. Electrocution was another way they got me to go to another level of consciousness. Sugar coma and other drugs injected into my body altered my consciousness. Stimulating my genitals over and over without any release took me to another state of consciousness. This type of torture would cause so much pain, torment, changes in my body, and confusion that they caused divisions in my mind. The evil people know if they can get a person into a trance state, they can insert thoughts and ideas without them being aware. For example, in the video games, music, phones, and movies that people watch and use today, there are electrical frequencies inserted to get people to an altered trance state of consciousness. In that state, they accept all of what is transmitted into their mind. Arrival is a recent movie where I have seen this programming technique played out. In this sci-fi movie, there were aliens that arrived on earth. They had a language that looked like different variations of the letter O. This is a common symbol of the Illuminati. The language of the aliens was being measured by the sound waves and frequencies. The woman in the movie went into a trancelike state to receive a gift from them. The gift was to be able to see the past, present, and future. She was in a trance. At that point, there is a sound wave language that is not understood by our conscious mind but is understood by our unconscious mind. So the subliminal messages are sent electronically to other parts of the consciousness. Have you ever seen a child who has played video games for so long they don't hear, see, or notice anything around them? Have you ever seen a person so engrossed into a movie that they go somewhere else? Or have you gotten on a phone call and lost all track of time? Have you been on Facebook or some form of social media and realize hours have gone by? This is the same type of thing but a milder form. There are deliberately placed messages sent through sound frequencies. The mind has gone into a vulnerable trance state, so it is open to receiving these messages. I only share this so that God's children can all begin to be defensive about what we allow our minds to be open to. Also, so that we will pray that our minds will be so in tune with Papa God, that we will discern when messages that we do not want are trying to get through. This is the Illuminati's main way of communication. What if the Church could hear what the Illuminati is saying and know their next move? What if we could with the power of Papa God be able to shut down their frequencies and communication and cause an end to their plans? In the end, we win, but what about now? Shouldn't we, "the body of Christ," be as powerful as we can be? What if we could shut down evil at an unprecedented level, giving millions the opportunity to be free!

A scripture that describes how Papa God exposes evil is Ezekiel 8. I know this scripture is long, but I believe it's very important in learning how we can combat the evil people. Ezekiel 8:1–18 says,

> And it came to pass in the sixth year, in the sixth month, in the fifth day of the month, as I sat in mine house, and the elders of Judah sat before me, that the hand of the Lord GOD fell there upon me. Then I beheld, and lo a likeness as the appearance of fire: from the appearance of his loins even downward, fire; and from his loins even upward, as the appearance of brightness, as the color of amber. And He put forth the form of an hand, and took me by a lock of mine head; and the spirit lifted me up between the earth and the heaven, and brought me in the visions of God to Jerusalem, to the door of the inner gate that looketh toward the north; where was the seat of the image of jealousy, which provoketh to jealousy. And, behold, the glory of the God of Israel was there, according to the vision that I saw in the plain. Then said He unto me, Son of man, lift up thine eyes now the way toward the north. So I lifted up mine eyes the way toward the north, and behold northward at the gate of the altar this image of jealousy in the entry. He said furthermore unto me, Son of man, seest thou what they do? even the great abominations that the house of Israel committeth here, that I should go far off from my sanctuary? but turn thee yet again, and thou shalt see greater abominations. And He brought me to the door of the court; and when I looked, behold a hole in the wall. Then said He unto me, Son of man, dig now in the wall: and when I had digged in the wall, behold a door. And He said unto me, Go in, and behold the wicked

abominations that they do here. So I went in and saw; and behold every form of creeping things, and abominable beasts, and all the idols of the house of Israel, portrayed upon the wall round about. And there stood before them seventy men of the ancients of the house of Israel, and in the midst of them stood Jaazaniah the son of Shaphan, with every man his censer in his hand; and a thick cloud of incense went up. Then said He unto me, Son of man, hast thou seen what the ancients of the house of Israel do in the dark, every man in the chambers of his imagery? for they say, the LORD seeth us not; the LORD hath forsaken the earth. He said also unto me, Turn thee yet again, and thou shalt see greater abominations that they do. Then He brought me to the door of the gate of the LORD's house which was toward the north; and, behold, there sat women weeping for Tammuz. Then said He unto me, Hast thou seen this, O son of man? turn thee yet again, and thou shalt see greater abominations than these. And He brought me into the inner court of the LORD's house, and, behold, at the door of the temple of the LORD, between the porch and the altar, were about five and twenty men, with their backs toward the temple of the LORD, and their faces toward the east; and they worshipped the sun toward the east. Then He said unto me, Hast thou seen this, O son of man? Is it a light thing to the house of Judah that they commit the abominations which they commit here? for they have filled the land with violence, and have returned to provoke me to anger: and, lo, they put the branch to their nose. Therefore will I also deal in fury: mine eye shall not spare, neither will I have pity: and though they cry in

mine ears with a loud voice, yet will I not hear
them.

I'm wondering if the doors and walls that Papa God was talking
about to Ezekiel were realms and portals in the spirit. I pray that as
the powerful church of Jesus, we allow Papa God to help us see the
evil and expose it—that we take back the spirit realm that is ours
through the inheritance we received from Jesus!

In order to track me, there were microscopic electronic sensors that were implanted throughout my body so that they could
input information through frequencies anywhere in the world. Also,
these sensors tracked me everywhere I went and what I did. Rituals
were done to place DNA on each of the sensors and send out signals
demonically to make soul ties with each part of my body with other
people throughout the world. The soul ties with other victims allowed
the demons to stay. The soul ties gave them power to scramble and
cover the electronic signals and communication that was happening
throughout the world by the Illuminati. This is a way of communication a language that can't be detected by people. Unfortunately,
the church has been targeted to get them to walk in the natural more
than the spirit, so they are not aware of the electronic language. The
soul ties create a powerful demonic chain between victims throughout the world. I was tortured and told that if I was not "faithful" to
keep the chains, then the rest of the victims would die, and it would
be my fault. The physical implants were reminders that it was our
job to keep the secrets. Rituals were done where the people would die
when the implants were taken out. So we were tortured to believe by
seeing people die, that the implants had to stay in us. We had to keep
the implants and sensors a secret.

The programmers forced us travel in the spirit realm through
astral projection by taping our eyes open and making us look at
strobe lights and multicolored lights. Another way they forced us to
travel in the spirit is by spinning us around and around. This induces
a dream state just like in *Wizard of Oz*. While they are doing this
torture, at the same time, they would make different sound waves.
The sound of a heartbeat, triangle music instrument, and demonic

tongues were used like a Morse code unlocking the portal or lock in the spirit to the Illuminati eye. The Illuminati eye gets the person through the portal to go into another realm. The evil people use the victim's heart against them. The victim is told if they choose to go through the portal, they will have an opportunity to rescue people in the other realm. I found that this exact ritual is shown in the movie *Interstellar.* I love my husband, and he likes science fiction movies, so sometimes I endure them to bless him. I know I will end up getting healing from Papa God if anything surfaced during the movie. So in this movie, the daughter gets messages through Morse code, and she thinks it is a ghost. Her father travels in space to try and save the world by finding another place for people to live other than earth. During his travel, he is unable to complete his mission. So he is sent into a trancelike state. There are frequencies and sound waves that serve as the barrier between him and his daughter. He speaks to her in Morse code; it was him the entire time who was talking to her from the future. There are rituals set up exactly like that by the programmers. The father says the answer to communicating is *love.* The evil people said the exact same thing. To an Illuminati survivor, *love* is *evol* spelled backward. *Evol* was the word the evil people used to refer to the electric shock. This was used as torture specifically in the gravity machine as NASA. There have been many victims tortured in NASA with EVOL. This does not mean that everyone in NASA or anywhere is evil; it just states the truth that there are evil people in every area, government, entertainment, schools, and churches; and the list goes on.

The evil people programmed me with most of the scriptures, also with stories, words, and songs that had to do with Christianity. This was done so that when we heard anything at church, it would always be paired with some form of ritual and torture. The evil people know that the Bible is real and powerful. They just think they are more powerful. The word *covenant* meant sex in every situation with the Illuminati. To make a covenant, I had to have sex with someone, and then I was bound to them for life. I couldn't make the rape and torture end if I had a covenant, unless I died or they died. *Covenant* is a hideous terrorizing word for victims. I was told that God would not make a covenant with me, because I was too evil. So I had to have sex with Satan. I had to make a covenant with Satan to make me good enough. The covenant was formed through torture and rape. The meaning of the word *prayer* was also twisted. The evil people said "prey" was the true meaning of *prayer*. This meant that I had to kill someone or hunt them down to have the ability to talk to God. The programmers did this specifically so that when people say in church, "Let's pray," or "You need to pray," it is a major trigger. The evil people said that the church was trying to trick us to do evil things because it was a commandment to prey! The evil people set all of this up strategically so that none of what pastors or Christians say would be trusted, and the victims would think that the Christians were evil too. Prayer meant I had to find other victims as "prey," or they would find them and kill them. All I ever did was try every second of every day to find a way in the midst of all of the hell that people would suffer and hurt the very least. There was never a good choice. No matter what, I would choose the option that had the least amount of people getting hurt. In reality, I never had any options. They made me think I had options, but I never ever had a choice at all.

Fasting was used as a torture tactic. So when it was mentioned in church, I thought that God wanted us to be starved to torture us. They would stimulate my genitals over and over and say that I was out of control, and not give me food for weeks at a time. They said that without sex and food, I would kill people. When they would starve me, they said it was God making me fast. God was taking food away from me to starve me to get the evil out of me. Communion was also used to torture victims. There were demons that were summoned in and communed with while drinking human blood and eating human flesh. The evil people said that it was God's plan to try and make us good enough when He said, "Drink His blood, and eat His flesh." According to them, since Jesus didn't die for us, we had to have another sacrifice.

The Lord's Prayer was used to torture me and the other victims. I will walk through the entire prayer to show what they do with each phrase of the prayer. "Our Father," I was told we had no father, so we weren't included in this prayer unless I did the things God told me to do in the prayer. Our "father" was my programmer. That was the case with all the victims. They made me get on my knees and say, "Hallowed be thy name. Thy kingdom come." This meant I had to do oral sex on the person who was "father," and he had an orgasm in my mouth. "Thy will be done" meant he tortured me "on earth as in heaven." My programmers sent out the parts of my mind that were named after the physical parts of my body as they electrocuted each organ and astral projected them into the demonic realm. "Give us this day our daily bread" meant I had to eat human flesh, as they placed it before me. If I didn't eat the flesh, they told me that I would cause other people to die. "And forgive us our debts, as we forgive our debtors" meant that I had to have sex with people to be forgiven. So when people in the church say, "You have to forgive," victims think they are saying we have to have sex with them. They always told me my debt was never paid. That is why they had to put me in a cage. They said that Jesus wouldn't pay my debt. So they had to turn me over to the torturers and tormenters. They tortured me to believe I couldn't pay the ultimate debt and that there wasn't anybody who would pay the debt for me. "Lead us not into temptation" meant we were the whores and sluts who were tempting people with sex. "Deliver us from evil" meant if they put us in a cage, then they were rescuing other people from temptation, because we were evil. "For Yours is the kingdom, the power, the glory forever. Amen." The last sentence the evil people told me meant that they could masturbate us, and if we had an orgasm, we were saying we were God. So I thought I needed to be destroyed because I was so prideful and evil. At the end of the ritual, we had to bow down to our programmer and worship them because they kept us from being evil by torturing and raping us. We were told we had so much evil sexual feelings inside us that we had to go through all of that torture for us not to be evil. They showed us the Lord's Prayer and read it over and over, so we did not question it. It was what God said should happen to us, the only communication He had with us.

Also, John 3:16, which says, "For God so loved the world, that He gave His only begotten Son that whosoever believeth in Him will not perish but have everlasting life," was used in rituals to cause horrible isolation and fear. Since I was told that I was not a part of the world that God was talking about in this scripture, I was put in a room alone for a long period of time. They said that I was too evil to be loved by God and that He didn't even include me in His love. There were programmers who said they were God and Satan. Then they would have sex. After the people who said they were God and Satan had sex, during the ritual, they had a lady give birth to a baby. I was told it was God and Satan's child, because "begotten" meant they had sex. They forced me to touch the infant sexually, and they said that I would have eternal life because the baby's DNA would help me be chosen. I was just three or four years old at this time. After they made me do that, they said, "You're evil. You touched a baby sexually. We have to control you so you won't do that again." "You can't have eternal life, but if you try harder, you might be able to." Then they put me back in the cage and said I had to stimulate my sex parts to try to be better. I hated myself. I thought there was no other way for me.

Forgiveness was a trigger word for all victims. Forgiveness meant we had to pretend that the evil people were not evil, and we had to forget what they did to us. So every time a Christian says, "Forgive them," that means to us that we should pretend that they didn't torture us. So as you can see, the Christian words had opposite meanings for victims. That is why it is so hard to get free, and imperative that Christians are aware of what is going on. Without dealing with the truth, this just keeps the evil hidden and people in slavery.

Every time I had a Bible near me, they would say, "Open that GD Bible." I would open the Bible, and then I was forced to masturbate and read the Bible to get perfect. That was the only way I would be allowed to read the Bible. Every time I opened the Bible, I had sexual feelings. They said this was because I was so evil and perverted. The programmers would go on and would say, "Open the Bible wider, or you're never going to get there." They meant my legs and I would never get an orgasm. The orgasm meant I was perfect enough to be allowed to read the Bible. But when I had an orgasm, they said I was too evil to read the Bible and that I had made that up. Constant confusion and torment was what I faced every day. I didn't even have God to turn to, because I thought He despised and hated me. Since I would have to read the Bible while I was masturbating, then this made the Bible seem all about sex and very dirty. To "know" God or for God to "know" me meant I had to have sex. They would take me into a white room that was completely empty. Then a man that was named "God" walked in, all dressed in white. He wouldn't talk to me. He just raped me. Then I would hear a voice through a loud speaker that said, "You are banished. You are evil, and we have decided you deserve to die." The man whom I thought was God left, and I was there on the floor after being raped by whom I thought was God. They spoke on the loud speaker to make me believe it was God's voice that was talking to me. "Forget the past, and press on to the high calling of God." "You are called and chosen." At that time, other men were brought in, and they raped me. "This is your calling. Forget the past, and press on to the high calling of God." My calling from God was to forget and have sex with whomever they said. I tried and tried to do the best I could, because if not God said I should be dead. I had no idea that things could be different. If this was what God was like, then I was doomed. I was torn within. Why would God do this to me? Was I evil because I didn't like this? I thought I was.

The Scripture 1 Corinthians 9:24, which says, "Do you not know that in a race all the runners run, but only one gets the prize? Run in such a way as to get the prize," was used to get the victims to think that we were all in competition with each other constantly. The goal was to be the "one," and the person who ended up with "Jesus" was the "one." Their prize was that they would be controlled by their husband, who was chosen for them. Their chosen husband would be Jesus to them. This allowed them to win the prize of heaven. Every single thing I did was to strive to be good enough. Even the cars that passed as I was driving were in competition with me, they said. So there was no middle ground: either you stayed on the right side of the road and went very slow to make sure you were last, or you had to speed to get to first place. But we never were the first or the last. We were always in the "middle," those who did not get to go to heaven. In the rituals, the evil people would kill a person at the finish line and say it was my fault because I didn't go fast enough.

The evil people would recite Philippians 4:8 (NIV): "Finally, brothers, *whatever* is true, *whatever* is noble, *whatever* is right, *whatever* is *pure*, *whatever* is *lovely*, *whatever* is *admirable*—if anything is excellent or praiseworthy—think about such things." The programmers said they loved me while they raped me. Every evil they did, they paired it with something that was supposed to be good. This caused great confusion. I was tortured and forced to focus on the pretend things and forget the bad, because if I didn't, that meant I was evil. Papa God had to show me very clearly in my healing journey that I had to look at the evil they did to me. I had to see the lies that they told me to know the truth and be healed. How can you be healed if you don't even know what you're healed from? This is an extreme example, but it is true for every person. If you have feelings and emotions but you don't have any idea where they are coming from, Papa God wants to show you and then show you the truth where there are lies you believe. It brings supernatural peace and healing when Papa God speaks truth!

The evil people started in Genesis to pervert and twist my mind about God and creation. They said the expanse was the penis and the water was our body. The earth was formed through sex between Satan and God. The vibrations on the earth was to cause us to have sexual feelings. So God was forcing us to have sex with Him. They would put vibrations to my sexual part to make me have sexual feelings and tell me that God was having sex with me. All of what I saw that was made by God, I was programmed to believe, was sexual. Even the stars, they said, were made to remind me that God made the earth through sex. They said God separated the day and night in order to separate the good and evil people. When the sun rises, that is supposed to be God being stimulated to have sex with us.

The seasons of the year were for evil people to bring out different parts of my mind to torture. There are always corporate rituals at each season change. The programmers would spin me around over and over to cause my mind to disassociate, and they would say over an over that God spins the earth around to cause us to forget. Papa God has had to take every single lie and show the truth that He made the earth to show us that He loves us. Now Papa God is always showing me His genuine love through His creation. I was always forced to bond with animals, and then they would kill them. I wasn't as afraid of animals as I was of humans. It always seemed like animals liked me until the evil people tortured the animals to turn on me. That rejection by the animals, even though the animals were being tortured to do things to me, was a horrible feeling.

I seem to always feel close to Papa God when I see sunsets, animals, birds, and beautiful scenery. These are Papa God's signs to me each day that I'm free! For example, I was getting some healing from a memory one day, and I was sitting in my car. There was a tree nearby, and a leaf fell off the tree. He said, "You are not connected to the evil people anymore." So every time I see a leaf floating to the ground, that reminds me that I'm free!

In the first five years of my life, I had been in this "hospital" setting and had no outside influence at all. During that time, they set up pictures where we looked like a happy family. The reality was they were programmers posing as parents. When I walked out of the hospital and went outside for the first time, I saw a yellow flower and a yellow butterfly. I remember genuinely thinking that there must be something better something else other than the torture I was enduring. I had a tiny grain of hope planted that maybe God was not evil and that He didn't hate me. The programmers looked at me and the change in my expression when I saw the yellow flower, and they said, "God didn't make any of this for you. This is not even real for you. This is only real for the people that are perfect." Even after telling me that, the truth is that that was a life-changing moment for me, the very first moment that I saw of glimpse of God, that made a lasting impact on my life. The Word says, "I tell you, if they keep quiet, He replied. Even the rocks will cry out" (Luke 19:40). So if Papa God can use rocks or a small flower to speak, He can use your life powerfully!

Chapter 9

Their "Product"

"Beloved, do not believe every spirit, but test the spirits
to see whether they are from God, for many false
prophets have gone out into the world." John 4:1

By age five, the foundational programming was complete. Scientifically, it is proven that our belief system is primarily fully formed by the age seven. Now it was time to reveal their "product." That is what they called the victims they program. Their next plan was to get me to believe that the United States was the best place in the world and that there truly was an "American dream." They put me on a private plane, and I had no idea where I was going. I was in a cage. If I was taken out the of the cage, I was on a dog leash. As horrible as that was, I was glad to be some person's property because I was terrified of myself. All of the programming had made me wonder every second what I would do if I wasn't somebody's property.

The programmers gave the denial parts of my mind names like Perfect Princess, Sugar Queen, and Stupid. They made sure that my legal name sounded like a devil and demon, so anytime they said my name, I knew that my real name was devil and demon. All of the children's names in the house where we were started with the letter *D*. So with these legal names, we could each play the role and program of devil, demon, and denial. The main programmers' names started with *R*s. *R* and *R*. They would say, "The only rest and relaxation you get is through us. We keep you from doing evil. You can only rest when we are in control or torturing you." The lies would continue. "You have to work every second to be good when we are not around. God created you to work every second. God says you have to read the Bible to see how evil you are. We just want you to rest, and the only rest God says you get is to forget, to have sex, and torture." They reinforced these lies by making me clean up after every ritual. I had to clean up all of the blood and body parts and anything else they said to clean. If there was a speck or spot or even if there wasn't, they would make it look like there was. I couldn't ever clean well enough. Then they would trash every single thing I did and make me start over. This would go on for hours and hours. There was never ever rest for me. I was working 24/7. Even in the few hours that I did sleep, I was in torment because I was afraid I would kill someone in my sleep.

Flatliners is a movie that is a ritual-based movie. In the movie, they deliberately get their heart to flatline. Just like the movie, the programmers hooked me up to an electrocardiogram. They would shock me until I would pass out, and before I passed out, they would show me that my heart was flatlining. As they showed me that my heart had flatlined, they would say, "We have control of whether you live or die." They would take me to places in the spirit realm while I was flatlining, a place they called heaven and hell, and do programming in those places. Then when they revived me, they said that they kept me from doing evil. I was terrified not to have them. This fear brought an influx of demons that formed a demonic bond with the programmers.

When they flew me to India, I had no idea where I was. I was put in a room by myself. I was not given clothes, my head was shaved, and they poked my eyes with needles to make them look red. There were rats and insects everywhere. I was in torment as the rats and the insects crawled all over me. There was no relief from the torture. As I sat there in excruciating pain, there were Indian men who were dressed in military uniforms, and they would come into the room. They screamed at me and raped me over and over. There was no one to help me. I had no hope; I believed I was going to die. The fear of death was intense because of the programming that they had done about death. For me, death was a much worse fate than living. there was no rest in death. There was just killing to do because I had no person to control me. At that point in the torture in India, the people who programmed me from conception walked in. The programmers had already put layers and layers of denial and false bonding to make me cling to them. For example, since they had killed the lady who was my mom and said it was my fault, they said, "You don't have to be your mom's killer if you just pretend like I'm your mom. The pain will go away, and you will have a pretend mom. That is better than having no mom." My programmers said that I could have the "American dream." If I pretended that none of the torture ever happened, they would take me to America and I could have a life there. I soon found out that there is no such thing as the "American dream."

The deepest level of denial was the torture where the programmers made my sexual parts programmed to be aroused at the most hideous things. They would stimulate my genitals and then bring an infant into the room. They would do this over and over until sexual arousal at the presence of the infant was an automatic response. This was used as another layer of denial. It was programmed into my mind that if I said clearly that the programmers are good, then they would not tell people I was a child molester. I thought because they had trained my sexual parts to be aroused when an infant was brought into the room that that meant I was evil and a child molester. There were double binds constantly being put in place to cause my mind to give up and choose the lesser evil between the two options. The definition of a *double bind* is only having two horrible options. This was always the constant state in my life. Another example of a double bind was when the programmers would say, "If you molest them, you don't have to kill them. Wouldn't you rather them go to heaven and not hell?" The programmers said that if I killed the children, they would go to hell and be evil all their days because my spirit would take them over. If I molested them, they would go to heaven, and the programmers would make sure that my spirit didn't take them over. Either way I looked at it, I was evil, and I was going to have to do something bad, but I always tried to choose the lesser evil. The reality is that I never chose anything. I was forced to do things—physically, mentally, spiritually, and emotionally forced! I never had a choice! This locked the denial into my mind. Of course, I never ever would want anybody to know those evil things about me. And my programmers said they would keep it a secret if I choose to never turn on them and say that they were evil. The programmers had to be "the perfect family" in my mind, or they would tell the truth about who I was to everybody. They would send me back to India or to the hospital, and I didn't ever want that to happen. There was terror constantly!

Another country they sent me to was Africa. The goal of sending me to Africa was to seal a foundation of false importance, false gifts, and false power. They had me play the role of the queen of the Africans. This meant that every man "wanted" me and wanted to have sex with me. As the African programmers were raping me, I felt like I was to blame because they kept saying, "You want this. You want this power." The confusion was that somewhere inside, I did want the power to have someone want me, because no one had ever wanted me or chosen me. I hated myself. The programmers said I was completely evil because I wanted them to be my sex slaves. I just believed what they told me. I was treated like an animal, not adored for who I was; I was used for sex. The Illuminati said that because I was a mixed breed, I could save the Africans and give them some blood other than dog blood. And then when they raped me, my programmers said I was less than a dog. So no matter what I did, I was always treated as less than human.

The objective of the Illuminati was to make me hate all other nationalities other than those in the Illuminati bloodline. The Illuminati wanted me to see that all people who were not Illuminati were trying to make me look bad and destroy me. The programmers wanted me to hate all nationalities by convincing all of the parts of my mind that I was hated by everyone who is of different nationality. If the programmers could do that, then they could keep a foundation of denial in my mind about America—the foundation of denial that says, "America is perfect, and I live in America, so I'm perfect, and my family is perfect." One of the ways the programmers did this was by lining up Jewish people in front of me and saying that they had to be a sacrifice. If they were not a sacrifice for all of the other people, I would have to strap a bomb to my chest where my heart was and blow up thousands of people. So I had to choose between blowing up thousands of people and killing a few people and saving thousands. The only way that I would not be a killer for eternity was to do what they said. So I was physically forced to do what the evil people said. I was trying to find the lesser evil choice. The programmers said that the Jewish people who were lined up in front of me would go to heaven because they were a sacrifice. They told me that God was planning on sending them to hell, but by doing this, I would be saving them from hell. I was torn by grief in my core like the ripping of flesh from a person's body. I believe that the physical pain would have been easier than the torment I had to endure emotionally.

They took the symbols of the crescent moon, the sun, and the tree; and put them together to form a symbol that they used in rituals. If you look at the archdiocese logo, you will know they use the same symbols. The archdiocese is linked specifically to the Illuminati and Islam. In the rituals, the goddess Isis and the sun god Rah were used to create a demonic stronghold. The programmers took the blood of the people whom they beheaded and poured their blood all over me. I wanted to die because of the torment and pain this caused me. But I was more afraid of death. I was afraid of the evil that the programmers said I would do after death. This "programmed fear" executed by the Illuminati was to keep me from killing myself. They planned it that way so they would not lose the time and money that they had invested in my programming. If I killed myself, that would be a loss to their rank in the Illuminati, meaning their programming had failed. During the Isis rituals, the programmers also brought a child into the room, and they told me that it was my child. I never knew if the children were mine or not, because they always killed or took my children from me. When they brought in the child they said was mine, they told me that my child had to be a sacrifice too. The programmers said there had to be an adult sacrifice and a child sacrifice. The sacrifice was needed because Jesus didn't die for us. I had to have a sacrifice that was not Jesus. The evil people took the sword they used to behead a person and forced my hands onto the sword and forced the sword into the child's heart. I was way beyond the capability to handle this pain and devastation, so my mind divided into thousands of pieces. I was told that if I was a "faithful one," my child would rise again. They said that my sacrifice at the end would cause him to have life instead of death. All of the soldiers, the programmers called the "faithful ones." We were told that we would be joined together at the end. Since I had a sacrifice, I had earned the right to only have to kill a few people at the end. I would have a bomb strapped to me at the end and blow myself up, instead of having to blow up thousands or millions of people. At the end, I would have a sacrifice and end up being a virgin. Therefore, my eternal fate of being evil and killing people, like the programmers said, would be over finally. The evil people continually tried to use the conscience and love that Papa God put within me to torment me and use it against me.

After the different foundational programming throughout the world was complete, the programmers were ready to begin the infiltration of their "product" into society. I was taken to a very small town in Kentucky. The town had a German name. My role had been programmed into me since I was born. I was the "Kentucky girl." There was another boy that was brought to the same house that I was taken to, and when we were around people, the programmers said he was my brother. When we were alone, the programmers said he was "my Jesus." They tortured me and forced both of us to mate. The programmers tortured him to believe that he had to control me, so I wouldn't be evil. Our programmers forced us to believe that they gave us to each other because we were so evil that we needed each other to get the evil out of us. By having sex all the time, we were told we were purifying our blood. So they intentionally created a strong bond between us. Then they brought in other people whom we would have to have sex with in front of each other. They would tell each of us individually that we were evil and disgusting for having sex with our siblings. The programmers warned us that people couldn't ever know about it, or they would put us back into the hospital that we were born in. They also would pit us against each other.

They told me that he said I was fat and ugly. They told him that I was disgusted with him. When they did this programming against each other, they put us in a glass room so we could see what was happening to each other. They had speakers in the room that broadcast what they wanted us to hear. They said that this was the voice of God. So we had no one to trust. They never allowed us to get too close to each other or anyone, because we might get free.

Chapter 10

School

"To the pure, all things are pure, but to the defiled and
unbelieving, nothing is pure; but both their minds and
their consciences are defiled. They profess to know God,
but they deny him by their works. They are detestable,
disobedient, unfit for any good work." Titus 1:15-16

The school I was put in was a programming site. It had a German
origin and roots. The programmers had keys to the school. The
male programmer was a teacher, a coach, and a counselor at the
school. The Illuminati set up specific corporate sites in towns, cities, and states. These sites were for programming and experiments.
Eventually, they said that those sites would be used for concentration camps for those who did not have the "perfect" Aryan bloodline. When the rituals were done in the school, it created a demonic
grid for the Illuminati to channel in demons. This location was
strategically chosen to maximize the amount of demons and power
that could be brought through the portal that they had established.
Portals are established on a global scale to control people's minds in
that area. This portal is established by torturing a person through
electric shock till they ask for the demons. The reason the victims ask
for the demons is there is no other way to get them to stop the torture. There are no other options. The programmers electrocuted my
head, and the pain was so intense that I sometimes would faint. This

type of torture causes divisions in the mind of the person, and they specifically create parts to hold the demons. I was told the demons were my friends and that they would take the pain away. There is a legal right created for the demons to be there, because the evil people had gotten my will through torture to submit to the demons to allow them in. Another way the programmers get victims to accept the demons is by threatening to kill someone if they do not accept the demons. We are promised that the demons will protect the person who has been threatened. When the demons have more power, more torture is done. When there is human sacrifice and rape, the demons strengthen, and the programmer gets more power.

I went to a school that had kindergarten through twelfth grade in the same building. They were doing experiments concerning torture and how the brain works there. The experiments were to see how the brain functioned and how they could control my brain and other victims' brains more. For example, they would tell me that my brain was responding like the brain of a pedophile, and then they would show me a screen with a brain that lit up when showed a picture of a child, and then they paired that with sexual stimulation. They said that my brain lighting up was proof that I was sexually stimulated by a child, and, therefore, I was a pedophile. I was terrified of myself because I thought I was an evil pedophile. They said that they would torture and rape me to keep me from doing evil to children. I thought I needed them to control me and that I had to have them so I would not be a pedophile.

The Illuminati uses the *Wizard of Oz* programming as a foundational program. The Illuminati represents the wizard, the New World Order. Every detail of the *Wizard of Oz* was used for torture. The rainbow was the denial overlay of the demonic realm. The evil people said the rainbow was a sign that God hated the mixed breeds and would destroy us if we did not perform perfectly. During one of the rituals, they poured bubblegum-smelling pink liquid on me, and I had to click my heels to get "over the rainbow." There was a machine that was used to stimulate my genitals over and over. I was told that if I achieve an orgasm, I would be allowed in Oz. Dorothy was in a dream state in the movie, and they would tell me over and over that all of the evil they did to me was a dream. I was tortured to believe that none of the torture, rape, and hell I went through was actually happening. They would give me drugs to make me feel disconnected and feel like I was in an altered state. This made me feel like I was going crazy. They said I would go crazy if I didn't stop thinking about what they did to me and just think about how perfect they were. They would stimulate my sex parts and say over and over that they were perfect. They said that I needed a new heart, mind, and courage. They would dissect a human in front of me and say it was my fault that they died. The organs were taken out of the person and planted within other people to form a blood tie with the people who died. They said that there was always Oz behind the curtain, watching to see what I did, and they would expose me if I tell anybody what was happening to me. The monkeys were represented as demons. The victims were told that we are monkeys with no genetic purity and who are completely evil. A part of my mind that was divided was named Monkey. I was forced to pick at people's skin and head like a monkey does. Oz was a specific language they had in the spirit realm. They communicated in different frequencies so they would not be heard or found out in the natural realm. This entire book is about evil. To follow the yellow brick road meant to follow the denial to the end until the New World Order takes over and gives the mixed breeds a new heart, mind, and courage to carry out the plans of the Illuminati.

There were German "Grand Mother" and "Grand Father" positions. I was supposed to take over the Grand Mother position as an elite if I married who they set up for me to marry. The programmers said that was the only way I would be pure enough. They looked like normal grandparents in society, but the torture with them was hideous. They dressed in military uniforms when not in public. They had a basement that had an old furnace in it, and they would burn people alive in it. They lived beside a railroad track, and he worked on the railroad. They said they would send me back to India to the train if I was not perfect enough. There was complete isolation in India, and they had created a whole system in my mind of denial about America. The Grand Mother would give me sugar bread for the sugar programming to take over, and then they would take me in the back room with body parts lying around all over the room and rape and torture me. I was terrified of that room. She said I could have a pure descent if I performed well enough. She would buy the specific clothes and makeup that the buyers wanted me to wear and then sell me "to make her money back," she said. I was prepped by bringing up the parts that had the ability to act the way she wanted me to act. Then they would sell me to the German programmers whom they were working with. The town that they were in were also concentration campsites, and there were many German programmers there.

The other programmers posing as grandparents also did a lot of military programming on me, as well as Native American rituals. They would scalp people and filet their bodies. As they did this evil, they called in demons to cover the evil they were doing. When you see people in places of influence speak to people, they are calling in demons and asking the demons for trances to fall upon the people so they will not detect the evil words that are being said to them under the surface. The demons cover their evildoing, making it all possible. The demons are channeled in, and people see a veil, instead of who they really are. They had a garage where people were worked on like cars, dissected and put back together. The male programmer's cover was a mechanic. It's important to know that these people hide in every area of life; they are doctors, lawyers, teachers, pastors. They choose to do this anywhere they can cover up what they do. The demons influence the minds of people during the trances to introduce the evil people's thoughts and ideas into their minds. The trance causes the people to go into denial, and they do not perceive anything about the evil that is going on. It numbs the people so that they are constantly in a fog of denial.

There were two people who posed as my aunt and uncle. They lived on a farm that had racehorses. This was in the wealthy racehorse section of Kentucky. They had gated land, with a large farm and fake bed-and-breakfast that was used for programming. They took me to the horse races and sold me to the buyers who were looking for Southern programmed victims. There would be people who flew in from all over the world to buy people, not horses. They were also there to test the "Kentucky programming." They were looking for girls who were able to be the southern sickening sweet denial role that the men would want to purchase. The people who posed as my aunt and uncle were very involved in the political system and drug cartel in Kentucky. There were police officers who were involved in covering up all of what was going on at the horse races, because they were paid a high price. They created a false pride within the victims through the high price they were sold at. In reality, we were treated like animals. They gave us dog commands, and we wore dog collars. We walked on a stage naked and were auctioned off. They rated us with numbers. If we did not do well in the auction, they put us in coffins and said that we were better off dead, that is, if we couldn't earn money for them. When I got a high price, they said I was prideful and showing off, and tortured the other girls because they said I was prideful. I hated myself for liking that I was sold at a high price; I just wanted some person any person to genuinely love me. Unfortunately, that would never happen until I was in my late twenties. The bed-and-breakfast that the programmers ran had a code name and was where programmers and traffickers could test out their product.

The other programmers who posed as my aunt and uncle were evil too, and they had other victims in their houses. There was another girl my age and a boy a couple of years younger, and they were supposed to be my cousins. I was pit against the girl. She had blonde hair and blue-green eyes, and they said she was a pure breed. So in the denial world, the everyday world, the programmers were pretending to be a normal family. In this pretend life that people saw daily, the programmers told me that I could be better than my cousin if I pretended well enough. They made sure I knew that she was always better in the Illuminati world, the world where bloodline was of upmost importance. She was better with the torture, rape, and programming. We were always in competition with each other. They said she was smart and I was stupid. If I acted stupid enough, they promised me that I wouldn't have to do the torture on other people that they forced me to do. They never kept that promise, of course. They said that I didn't have to do the torture if I would just try to make the other girl angry with me. I was told that if I faked being stupid she would live. She thought I was acting stupid, so she would have to do the torture.

Every single victim is programmed against each other. They don't want to take the chance that we would feel genuine love from each other. They were aware that genuine love would destroy their programming. They knew the truth. They knew the Word in detail and rejected it, because they wanted to be God. There was a boy whom we had to compete to get as a "Jesus" sacrifice for us. This person, they told us, was the one who would cover our sins. They called me "precious," and that meant that the core of my being was like Gollum, the evil creature in *The Lord of the Rings* who was taken over by the ring. The ring was the goal, and this meant sex. The other programmers who were the last posing aunt and uncle were in charge of getting me sexually where I was supposed to be. She would say she was a victim, and then they would act like they were raping her. I felt sorry for her. She said, "If you feel sorry for me and I'm the victim, then I will show you how to be the best at sex." I thought she was sincere, but she would laugh at me when I had sex and say, "I'm the victim because you're so evil." She told me that if I said she was the victim, I was allowed to stay looking young, like she was. They called demons in to slow my aging, and I was told I would be left alone if I cease to be salable, so I received the demons.

The evil people had already set up programming to cause division in my mind and for me to think I had a twin. This was done to cause complete division between the left and right side of my brain and body. I was tortured to believe the left side was evil and the right side was the perfect princess (denial). They told me that I was a twin—that there was a good twin and an evil twin, and I was the evil twin. There was a girl who was posed as my best friend by the evil people. The programmers dressed us alike and made us look alike. She was a victim from birth also. She was supposed to be the good twin. We were constantly made to be in competition with each other. If she was better at something, then I was tortured and put in a room by myself until "I got better." Every second, they would say she's prettier, smarter, better than I was. This caused a love-hate relationship because I thought she was my sister. They told me that I was always labeled the evil person. She was tortured to believe the same way. Her programmer was the secretary at the school we went to, and she was the gatekeeper. The reason her programmer was called the gatekeeper was she scheduled the reprogramming and watched to see how the programming was holding up in school.

When they established a specific programming, we were turned over to another programmer. This programmer was a gymnastics coach. There were many victims he was programming under the disguise of a gymnastics instructor. There were victims who had to compete in gymnastics and get specific ranking from their performance. We were pit against each other on purpose; the instructor had a large sex trafficking business with the gymnastics as a cover. We were taken to competitions and shown as animals doing tricks to see if people wanted to buy us. He took us to a corporate gymnastics camp that had German coaches that were involved with the programming. He was one of my main programmers since age five and continued to be so until my twenties. Since my programming was based on the lie that I was evil, they never allowed me to get too good at anything, including gymnastics. They said I would be too prideful and begin to think I didn't need them anymore to keep me from being evil.

At age five, they took me to a small Baptist church in that town and began to pretend to be active members of the church. The female programmer was disguised as a children's minister, and the male programmer managed the church's cemetery that was at the end of the road where their house was. To people, they looked like normal parents, and no person ever questioned that. There were other people in the church who were programmers that were doing the same thing to me and other victims. The programmers in the church passed the victims back and forth between them, trying out their techniques. I was made to sing in front of the church; this terrified me. Because during the rituals, I had to sing for all of the evil people, and they would score me. If I didn't sing well enough, they would hurt people. I would shake because I was so afraid, and my voice would tremble. They always said I wasn't good enough, and people got hurt. The pastor at that church started getting to close to me, so they focused on taking him and his wife down. They began to slander him within the church. The female programmer had the key to the parsonage under the disguise that she was taking care of the parsonage for the church. She would do rituals with torture and rape when the pastor and his wife weren't there. They would put the pastor's picture up in front of me while they were torturing me, and they would say that he was really the person that was torturing me. They said over and over that he had told them to do what they were doing. They also told me the pastor and his wife had a mentally handicapped daughter whom they had put in the mental hospital because they didn't want her. They said that I was the mentally handicapped daughter they were referring to. The programmers in the church started telling everybody that's the pastor's wife was a whore, and that she was trying to have sex with all of the people in the church. They were setting a foundation to destroy the pastor. They made sure they had a backup plan, that if my programming ever started breaking down, they would have a "fall guy."

The evil people showed me the Jesus video. Each detail of Jesus's life was perverted for me. The programmers said when Jesus came to earth, He had sex with Satan and expected all of us to do the same. The evil people said Jesus was not raised from the dead for me. So I had to try and get the men who were dressed like Jesus sexually excited so that they would be "raised" from the dead. The "Holy Spirit coming" was a sexual experience according to the programmers. This was when the Holy Spirit would ejaculate in your mouth, and then you had to speak false tongues of demons. They would hang us up on crosses and say we had to stay there until we were good enough for Jesus to die for us, and we never were. They did rituals in the pastor's office, because they had the key to the church. During these rituals, they put pictures of the pastor in front of me. They said that when I went to see the pastor, I had done evil things. They did the rituals with the cross in the church, and they would hold me under the water in the baptismal and say that they could only let me up when I was saved, "perfect." So since I couldn't be perfect enough, they pretended like they gave me an alternative. They did sexual things under the water to make me have an orgasm; that meant I was perfect and saved. My programmer was the overseer of the cemetery for the church. They would put the remains of people in the holes for burial without anyone ever knowing. They also had a tombstone for a child that was supposed to be my brother, whom they said I killed. The programmers said that I shouldn't have been born. He should have been born. They couldn't get their way and be in control at the church, so the evil people ended up getting the pastor fired, and they replaced him with someone from the cult.

There was another child who was brought into the house as well. They told me I was his mom, even though I wasn't old enough to be his mom. I took care of him and was like his mom. I bonded with him because I took care of him daily, and then they forced me to have sex with him. He had blonde hair and blue eyes; they said he was of pure descent. They forced me to be his handler. That meant that I had to hurt him, and if I didn't, they would hurt him much worse. This was the most hideous type of torture because they used my heart that chose Papa God against me. I would rather have been tortured myself, then be forced to hurt him. I was given no choice. He was forced to be very quiet. It made me angry because they told me that he was being quiet because he feared me because I was so evil. They said he was always trying to tell me I was evil by being silent. I was only allowed to sleep in the doghouse behind the house, even though they had a room "for show" in the house that was supposed to be mine. I was treated worse than an animal. If I performed sexually, I was allowed out of the doghouse. I was kept in isolation there, with no food and with bugs and mice crawling on me. If I didn't act perfectly, they would threaten to put me back in the doghouse. The threats would be that they would kill the kids at school and the other victims if I didn't pretend like things were perfect. Also, there was a place under the stairs in the garage that I would have to stay sometimes. When they allowed me to be in the house, I had to be doing something like cleaning or having sex or whatever they told me I had to do. I would sleep in the baby bed of the little boy who was supposed to be my child but only if I had sex with him. He was used as leverage against me constantly, and I would do what they wanted if they would not hurt him.

The programmers put me in pretty, pink princess pageants and forced me to pretend that all was perfect. They bleached my hair in the sun and made me look blonde, and said if I acted perfect enough, I would earn my way to heaven. I won a beauty pageant, and there was another victim who was chosen to be in the pageant with me, and she lost. The other boys who were in her house were forced to rape me; that is what they said I got for winning. The girl who lost the pageant ended up getting the boy I couldn't have, because she was a pure breed. This was a boy who was blonde and had blue eyes, and they called him "the divine." He bred with me and the girl they called my twin, and we had to compete for him. He never liked or chose me they said, because I was too evil. He only used me for sex. My programmer would have sex with him in front of me and say that I was too evil, fat, and ugly for him to ever want me.

The evil people channeled in demons and asked for the power to shape-shift into werewolves during rituals. They would call for the demons to take over them and shift them into the form of a werewolf. They would search for prey. They would kill and eat what they killed. This is shown clearly in the ritual movie *Wolf,* where the man is chained down to keep him from shape-shifting during the night, and doing evil things in the night. He always gets loose and is able to go kill. They would make me wear a werewolf mask, and they told me that I was evil. They said I would get free so they had to shape-shift to keep me from doing evil. The terror that I felt when I saw the demons possess them and their entire being shift into a werewolf was unspeakable. I was terrified of myself most of all, though, because I thought I was a werewolf. I thought that was my core, and I thought I was uncontrollable. I didn't want to be evil. I wanted to genuinely love people and be kind to people. They made sure I was petrified of myself. Since I had already chosen Papa God at my core, I belonged to Papa God. The demons didn't take over me and make me shape-shift into that being, but I didn't know that truth. I also saw them shape-shift into a creature that looked like Gollum in *The Lord of the Rings.* They would crawl around like an animal. They said that was the core of who I was, and when they weren't around to keep me under control, that was what I looked like. They continually said they were only doing what they were doing to show me how evil I was. They said my evil nature made them do what they did. They said that the evil within me possessed them and caused them to shape-shift into zombies and vampires that ate people and drank their blood. I never questioned what they said, because ever since I was born, I had been shown dead people that they said I killed while I was asleep. I would wake up, and there would be dead people all around me, and then they showed me videos of someone who looked like me doing evil things. This was how they kept me under their control for so long. The movies and TV shows today are just desensitizing people to the fact that there are really people who do these things daily in this country. Where do you think the entertainment industry gets the ideas for the movies? This really happens; it's not a movie.

The evil people have knowledge of the way the brain and body works, since some of them are chemists, biologists, neurologists, doctors, and scientists. The body has nerves that send electrical impulses to the brain, heart, and major organs that communicate what to do in the body. The evil people have had scientists for years studying how to control the nerves of a human being. They use the process of sending electrical impulses to try and control the entire nervous system. They have control over the person's body remotely. The Illuminati programmers use electricity for torture and control; rituals are done over the nerves and major organs to cause them to be under their control. There are demons that are assigned to the nerves to cause them to flex and react the way that the programmers want them to. This is also used as a major trigger, because they have convinced us as victims to believe that they are able to get us to do whatever they want us to do physically. When the mind believes a lie, the body is affected in how the body reacts. The evil people plant tiny electrodes in all of the nerves to send electrical impulses throughout the body creating migraines, pain in the victim's heart, and other physical pain. With being physically controlled remotely, they convince the victims to another degree that there is no way out.

At school, I had to act perfect, to play the role of the perfect princess. There were some teachers who were programmers, and the principal and assistant principal were programmers. This was a small elementary and high school (from kindergarten to twelfth grade). I was in the same building for twelve years. Each teacher I had each year was planned ahead of time so that every move I made was controlled. I had only denial friends (friends who were chosen for me), who were victims themselves. To anybody looking at us, they would have said, "That is a perfect family," but it was hell. I was trained to act the way they wanted me to act. I had to sit and watch hours and hours of TV and then act out what I saw. If I didn't perfect what I saw done by the actress on TV, I was tortured. Watching the TV was work. I had to memorize every move that was made and every word that was said. I had to be an actress in my life every second of every day. I was depressed and suicidal all the time, but nobody ever asked any questions the entire time. They saw a "family" involved in school, church, and normal activities that looked "good" on the outside. People would tell me that my depression was the result of my selfishness and spoiled nature. I was forced to be very active within the school as a cover for what they were doing to me. I was a cheerleader in band color guard, and I was voted band and basketball queen. I was never allowed to be the homecoming queen, because they said I was too evil. The word *home* meant sex, and if you had a "homecoming," you had an orgasm. They would stimulate my genitals over and over and over to cause a division in my mind and make me feel tormented, and never allow an orgasm. I was terrified of orgasms, because they would kill someone or electrocute them every time they allowed an orgasm. They would say, "You're evil," "You liked that," "You wanted that." I blamed myself for the person dying, and I hated feeling sexual. The sexual feeling meant death and torture and orgasms meant I was 100 percent completely evil.

The house they lived in was in front of cornfields where rituals were performed, just like in the movie *Children of the Corn*. The exact rituals from the movie took place. There was furniture in the house, but I was not allowed to sit on the furniture unless I had sex or if they were videoing me. At the end of the road was the church cemetery, and the *Texas Chainsaw Massacre* was another ritual that they would carry out. They would cut up the people from the rituals and freeze them in the huge deep freezer in the garage. Then they would cook them into meals and force us to eat them. They made meals with a lot of sugar and fried foods, food that would taste good and cause a denial reaction. This caused confusion because of what they used in the meals. Then after I ate what they gave me, they would say, "You just ate ___," and it was a dog that I had had to care for and bond with or a person that I had bonded with. They did that on purpose to convince me that I was evil and rip my mind into many different pieces because the pain and torment was so severe. Another movie that has rituals throughout is *Nightmare on Elm Street*. They would give me drugs to make me go to sleep, and then they would bring someone dressed like Freddy Kruger into the room, and I would be disoriented. The person would chase me in a building, and I could never get free. Finally, I would stop running because I couldn't run anymore due to the drugs. Then I would pass out. They would move me into the room that they set up to look like my room. I would wake up, and they would say I was crazy and that I dreamed all of what happened. I thought I was crazy. They would say over and over, "You're crazy. You don't even know what's real." They would lock me in a cage until I told them that I made all of that up and that I was crazy. Most horror shows are taken from rituals. Another movie with rituals used by the Illuminati is *Chucky*. They had dolls and stuffed animals that they would display in my fake room on shelves. There was witchcraft spells and voodoo that was spoken over each of the dolls, and they used them to hurt Christians. They named each of them after the people they were praying against. They would tell me that all of the Christians were trying to destroy me, and how much Christians hated me. They told me if I didn't do the voodoo over the Christians, they would tell everybody how evil I was. Then when they would force me to do the voodoo and curses, they would say that I wanted to curse the Christians and that I was evil to curse them. They said that I was like Chucky, and that no matter what I did, I wouldn't die; I would always be killing people. I have had many people say, "Why didn't you just kill yourself?" The reason I didn't kill myself is they told me that I would go to a place where I would kill people constantly and not have anybody to control me. I was more afraid of that than of staying alive and being tortured continuously.

Chapter 11

Reprogramming

"Everyone who does evil hates the light, and will not come into the light for fear that their deeds will be exposed." John 3:20

I was taken to Florida many times, and I had to walk the beach like normal vacationers do. Unfortunately for me, programmers and traffickers would watch me from the motel balconies. They would watch to see how well I performed and if they wanted to buy me. When they did purchase me, a ritual would take place, and they would "test" me out. This was a way that programmers showed off their project. If their programming stood up to the testing, then the programmers would get more power and prestige in the Illuminati. If we did not do well, our specific programmers would go into a room with the other programmers and act like they were being tortured because of us. A part would be split off intentionally to think that it was our responsibility to keep the programmers from being tortured. They would torture me with electrocution, at the same time, to reinforce that I was at fault. Then, afterward, I felt great guilt and shame for my programmers being punished for my behavior. I would be buried in the sand and left there overnight with only an opening for my mouth so I could breathe. There were marks all over my body from insects that bit me, and I was gasping for breath the entire night. I was petrified; then my programmers would come back to where I was and say, "will you be faithful?" That was a question that meant would we fight in the end? I said yes. My programmers just laughed and said, "You're crazy! We don't get tortured by anyone. We are not a mixed breed like you." I thought I was protecting them and they were just tricking me again. While at the beach, they also had remote locations where they took me to. I was always blindfolded while being taken to corporate rituals. This was so I wouldn't be able to tell anyone exactly where we were. There were cages that they put in the water with the victims in them. They picked locations where there were sharks swimming in that area. They opened the cages and told us to swim as fast as we could to the surface. I was in complete terror. I couldn't swim fast. They told us that if we ever told anybody about anything that happened to us, they would bring us back and let the sharks eat us.

On my sixteenth birthday, I was taken out of town to a hotel where there were corporate rituals done. There were many other victims that were taken there also. There were boys who were paired with us, and they said that if I didn't perform well enough in the ritual, I wouldn't get to have a Jesus who would rescue me. They dressed me up like a witch and forced me to cast spells and curse people on this night. If I didn't do what they told me to do, they said they would kill the other kids who were there. They said the witchcraft powers would give me control over myself from being evil, so I followed through and said what they told me to say. That night, they burned down the large garage that was behind their house, and they said that I did it. They said I wanted to be a witch and to curse people and that I was trying to cover up how bad I was. They were trying to give me a false sense of power like the witch in the *Wizard of Oz*. The witch had power over all of the "monkeys," demons, to do what she said, and see in the spirit what needed to be seen. If I stayed like Dorothy and forgot the truth about what the evil people were doing to me, I wouldn't have to die, and I could have power over the evil that I thought was within me. The truth was they were trying to get rid of evidence of the killings they did, with starting the fire in the garage. They said that there had to be a sacrifice at every birthday so that I would be allowed to keep on living.

The evil people would impregnate me purposely and cause me to bond with the baby. They would tell me I would get to keep the baby. Before the baby was fully formed, they would induce me and make me go through labor. There was a time where the baby boy's head was being born, and they cut his head off as he was going out of my body. They said that I was evil and I was Satan because of what happened to him. As I have gotten healing for this from Papa God, He has shown me He is holding my baby boy. And there will be a day when I will get to hold him! Over and over, they tricked me to accept the demons and spirits so they could have more power. The Illuminati witchcraft is what they use to cause me to have to go through tunnel after tunnel of consciousness to get to the Illuminati conversations that happen on different frequency levels.

The level of torture that I was put through to make me submit to the demonic was beyond what the mind can comprehend. I had to take the electrical power and demons, or they would kill children and slit them open and let their body parts fall out on me. Just writing that is hideous, but I experienced it. I do not tell this for shock value or to get attention. I tell the extent and details of the programming and torture because Papa God told me to. It may not be politically correct or something that gives me more creditability, but I'm not seeking those things. I want the darkness to be exposed and for every single victim to have an opportunity to be free from the terror of torture and slavery. I just want people to be free. If I didn't take all of the demonic, then I wouldn't be able to get the people put back together, the evil people told me. As I was allowing Papa God to heal this, He showed me all of the children dancing and laughing with Him in heaven completely free from pain. That gave me great comfort!

The programmers chose men who were victims for me to be paired with in high school. There was always an agenda behind this. One of the men was put there to bring competition between the girl victims. If we performed well enough, we were allowed to be his chosen one. There were always two worlds that we had to live in, the denial world and the Illuminati world. In the denial world, I was always paired with a man who controlled me. This was done so that the programmers would reinforce the denial "perfect family, perfect life." I genuinely wanted to be accepted and wanted by someone. They knew this, so they said if I pretended well enough, I would always be allowed to have the man to control me. In the ritual, Illuminati world, the man was always with another girl. I was never chosen. This caused jealousy and competition with all of the victims.

One of the men whom I was paired had an older brother who was the designated "fall" for a crime that was done by the police. The police in that small town were very involved in the rituals. There was a police officer who lived next to us so that he could be a "watcher," making sure that no one got close to the ritual site. He was involved with the hell I was going through. He made sure there were no calls to the police for any noise and alerted the programmers if there was anything and anybody that came near the house. The police in this town were benefiting financially for being involved with the Illuminati.

Another girl that they set me up against in high school was a girl who was blonde, and they told me she was pure breed. She always was put in competition with me to get the guy in the denial world. My programmers would say over and over I was losing my power in the denial world, that she was going to take over. So each guy they paired me with, they paired her with as well; there was constant turmoil. She was allowed to be with them for a long time, and I was only allowed to be with them for a few months. They said that was because I was too crazy and out of control.

I was taken to the Nashville airport the majority of the time, to fly to the rituals and to be trafficked. They would dress me up specifically to what the programmer and trafficker asked for, and I would walk up to the sidewalk of where people were dropped off for flights. The programmers and traffickers would see me and contact my programmers to let them know if they wanted to purchase me. Then I would be put on a plane. Nashville is a hub for traffickers. There were a lot of pictures taken of each victim who was brought to the airport, and the secret network decided who got which victim.

There are a lot of victims who are sent to Christian camps to be programmed. Christian camps are targeted by the cult because it is easy to blend in there. The programmers know who the victims from birth are, and they also target kids or teenagers who have been abused severely previously to the extent that their mind has split. The programmers have an opening in their mind through that division; then they can continue the abuse. They always bring in the victims from birth and force us to abuse the ones who are dis-associated so that if they ever remember, they will remember about the victims, not the perpetrators. This is done as leverage—another way to get the victims to do what they are forced to do. They paired me with another girl at camp. She was blonde and was pure breed, they said. We were put together to control each other and compete so we would be good enough in college. She lived in Tennessee, and they sent me there to be programmed before college. I was taken to a college there for a cheerleading college camp and ritualized there. They took me to restaurants in downtown Nashville to sell me. I was trafficked, ritualized, and sold on different Tennessee and Kentucky college campuses' to other programmers.

After high school, they sent me to a college with programmers in that area, taking over as my handlers. This college was a large university in Kentucky. All of my classes were chosen for me, with programmers that were posing as professors in them. Psychology was chosen as my major. So that I could see how the psychiatrists and psychologists label the things happening to me as symptomatic of paranoid schizophrenia. This was done to reinforce the fear that they would tell people that I was crazy if I ever told what was happening to me. There was a professor who was a programmer on that campus who used the Kegel exercises and theory in a human sexuality class. He was programming and torturing me and other victims. His pro-gramming was based on the programming of Kegel that they had already done to me as a child. They forced my body to feel sexu-ally stimulated and forced me to do the Kegel exercises over and over. This was done to get me to feel crazy when sexual feelings were forced onto me. The main programmers told me, along with the professor, that it was my fault; I wanted to be raped. So I thought that it was my fault he raped me. I was forced to join a sorority at this university. The sorority was connected to the masons and Illuminati. The girl whom I was programmed with and posed as my best friend was also a member of this sorority. We had to compete to see who would be the best in the sorority rituals. There were many victims within this sorority. A well-known jewelry and clothing distributor was the symbol that was used for the sorority. The mascot was the lion. "Satan" was the focus and leader of the sorority.

The girl whom the programmers used to pose as my cousin lived with me in the dorm. There was a war constantly between us. We had a demonic competitive program set up ahead of time. So we had to constantly be working to get better than the other. If we did not, we were told they would kill people until we improved. In every situation, I was constantly threatened that they would torture and kill my younger brother, to whom I had had to play the role of a mother. For most of the victims, we had to take care of boys who had to play the "Jesus" role for us.

My main program was the perfect princess programming. I had to make sure everybody thought my life was perfect and that I had the perfect family. I tried out for college cheerleader, and the director was a programmer. He said I needed to lose weight to be a cheerleader. Then the starvation began. They told me what I could eat and could not eat. I was allowed to eat apples to remind me of how evil I was. I was called Eve and judged for choosing to eat the apple. Also, I was allowed to eat pretzels. Pretzels represented the body of Christ and that I had to have sex with Jesus and every person in order for them to live. I was forced to drink Diet Coke because they said it was laced with cocaine and would control me to keep me from doing evil. Pizza was a big ritual symbol. Pizza meant a sexual act had to be performed on a child. You see, this symbol recently has been exposed through what most people say is a conspiracy theory called Pizzagate. It is very real, and there is an enormous Illuminati pedophile ring at the top of government.

The programmers picked a man for me to be with; he was my controller at college. His job was to have sex with me and make sure I didn't do evil things. He was a cheerleader also, so he was with me all the time. By this time, I weighed about ninety pounds. My programming was starting to break down. I was not able to keep the perfect princess programming going. The starvation was done to get all of the parts of my mind to remember being in the hospital. Then I would choose to continue to run the perfect programming. If I didn't keep the program running, they would send me back to the hospital where I was tortured in from birth. At this time, some of the memories began flooding back of the rape I endured. I couldn't see the faces, but my programming was starting to crumble a tiny bit.

The Grand Mother would have me write poems by different parts of my mind to see what I would remember. When I finished the poems, she would take me to her basement with the furnace and burn people alive. She said if I ever told anybody anything, I would be the reason people burned alive. My mind was forced to create new parts to push down what I had witnessed. The horror of seeing and smelling a human being burned alive is incomprehensible. The worst torture was seeing the pain they were enduring and not being able to do anything to save them. I blamed myself for writing the poems. I thought I had caused them to be in torment. She kept saying over and over that it was my fault. I was so confused because she told me to write the poems. She tricked me over and over; she said I wanted to write the poems and that I was lying that she did not ask me to write them. I thought I was going crazy. I never knew what was true even about my own thoughts and feelings, because of the programming. I was forced to write; then I was tortured about what I had written. It was a double bind, just like my entire life had been.

The evil people would say, "I'm going to kill ____. I'm going to hurt ____. It's your responsibility to protect them." Then I would be sent out into the woods to try to protect them from being killed. They would always find the person and kill them before I found them. Then they would say, "Didn't you hear me? I said I was going to kill them. You should have protected them. It was your fault that they were killed. I knew you were evil." I questioned my motives continuously. I asked myself all the time. I always thought I had an ulterior motive, that I had some evil core planning ways to manipulate and deceive people. Since I was an infant, this is what I have always been told about who I am.

The programming was reiterated daily. I was told I had to do "more." I had to have sex "more." I was a mixed breed, so no matter how much "more" I did, I always had to do "more." This meant rape every day all day. I had to be tortured and raped "more" because I could never be "more" for anybody. I was just always not enough. They would tie me up and chant "more" over and over and stimulate my genitals with a machine. They would stop the machine and start it over and over and over.

There was a new pastor who was brought into the Baptist Church; he was a programmer during my high school years and after. They did many rituals in the parsonage and behind the house. My programmers were working with them to do rituals to put the face of the pastor they got fired, in my memories. If I didn't see the pastor's face, I would be put back in the hospital where they put me when I was little. They assigned me a psychiatrist, who tortured me and took me to the children's psychiatric hospital in the same town of the college I went to. He did rituals in the back rooms of the psychiatric hospital. He would put smelling salts to my nose and hold me down, and he raped me over and over. He said that if I continued the princess programming and forgot all the things that were starting to surface, he would marry me and be my controller. They bonded me to the psychiatrist in terror by forcing me to have sex and be held by him. He took pictures with me and the children being forced to have sex at the children's psychiatric hospital and said that I wanted it. He said he would show people the pictures and put me in jail if I ever told the truth of what was going on. He gave me a lot of different medications to make me not remember things. I couldn't function any longer. The functioning parts of my mind were beginning to see memories and break down. I wasn't able to continue with cheerleading, sorority, and college. They scrambled to begin to reprogram and cover all of the memories I was starting to have. The girl from my childhood that was my "twin" and I were put in jobs at a children's psychiatric hospital. We were tortured with the children there. Our programmers also took pictures of us being forced to do sexual things to the children, but they said we did it because we liked it. They called us pedophiles. The pastor whom my programmers took down and that the evil people were programming me around had a sister that worked at this same hospital. They told us that the pastor and his wife had decided they wanted the "good twin." They arranged a marriage with one of their family members to infiltrate the pastor's family with the Illuminati. They said since I wasn't able to keep things together, I was the "bad twin" who was left in the hospital.

The first hospital they started to reprogram me in was in Kentucky, and I was paired with a Jewish victim. The reason they did this was to remind me of what they forced me to do to Jewish people. If I didn't stop the memories, they would tell everybody what I did. Then everybody would see that I was evil and make me stay in the hospital. I looked like I had an eating disorder. I was starving, binging, and purging. This was what the programmers were using to control me. The torture and reprogramming in this hospital slowed down the memories for a short time.

There were many Christian ministries that they took me to. They took me to programmers who were specifically targeting Neil Anderson and the Freedom in Christ model of deliverance. The Illuminati look for and study different ministries that are making a difference in setting people free. They begin to discredit and program victims around those ministries so that the ministry will not be able to have any power. The "I am" statements in Freedom in Christ were used specifically. I was strapped down and told that if the "I am" statements were true for me, then I had to take the God position. Being God meant I would be physically forced to make the decisions on who lived or died. They said that God kills people who don't perform well, and if I wanted to be like God, I would have to do the same things God did. So instead, they would read over me the opposite of the "I am" statements. If I believed that I was evil and opposite of God, then I didn't have to be forced to kill anybody or hurt anybody. They programmed me every second to believe that if I ever had any power or thought good things about myself, that meant that I would be out of control.

After reprogramming me in the hospital, they sent me to a different college. This college was infiltrated as well with Illuminati professors and board members; the man posing as my uncle was part of the board at this college. He had a network that he was selling me to in this town in Kentucky where the small college was. I was still getting drugged and programmed by the psychiatrist from the other college town at the same time. The psychiatrist was setting up different places for me to go to get reprogrammed. There was another male victim who was brought to pair me with at this college. He was a football player, and I was a cheerleader, so we looked like the perfect pair. He had to be Jesus for me and have sex with me all the time to make me good enough. They made our child alters bond to keep us together. This made us choose the demons and whatever they told us we had to choose, in order to keep each other from getting hurt. We always had to be in competition with other victims to be able to keep each other. They brought other girls to have sex with him and would say I was too ugly, fat, and evil for him to choose me. I kept falling apart, and the programming kept breaking down. New memories started surfacing. They continually reprogrammed me with the childhood pastor's face, voice, and pictures over the real memories so they could slander him and bring him down.

They took me to a large Christian hospital in Texas to reprogram me. They had planted a programmer in that hospital who tortured me. The Illuminati always targets Christian hospitals, camps, churches, especially spirit-filled praying churches. This programmer said that he was able to commit me to a mental hospital by saying I was paranoid schizophrenic. He said if I didn't stop remembering, I was going to be put back in the hospital that I was born in. They did rituals to bury those parts that were remembering. I was forced to take a lot of pills and try to kill the parts of my mind that were remembering the truth. The evil people said that I was taken to a hospital to pump my stomach to get the evil parts out and to stop them. The entire reason this was done was so they could call in more demons, because I had chosen to try and kill myself, they said. There were more demons assigned as "friends" to push the memories down. The evil people said the demons would hide the "truth" about me, that I was an evil monster.

Another hospital that they took me to was a well-known hospital in Louisiana. This hospital is supposed to be for sexual abuse victims and perpetrators. They told me that they were sending me there posing as a sexual abuse victim, but they told me the truth was

I was there because I was a perpetrator. There were other Illuminati victims there. A victim whose father was a judge was there because all of her memories were starting to surface. All of the parts of her mind were talking and sharing what had happened to her. They said if I continued to allow all of the memories to surface, I would go crazy and look like her. They were trying to destroy the rebellious parts so that I wouldn't start thinking I was able to be on my own. The psychiatrist I was assigned to at this hospital filmed me and forced me to do sexual things to other people. She said if I ever told anybody what was going on, she would show the videos to people and put me in jail where I belonged. She said that molesters were raped every day in jail, and there wouldn't be any end to the torture that I would endure. I was terrified every second of myself, and of them. I had to pretend like the psychiatrist was not evil or face those consequences. I let them bury my alters, and I vowed to them I would forget.

I was also sent to Houston, Texas, to another well-known Christian hospital. There was a programmer assigned specifically to me there. The programmer was physically handicapped and in a wheelchair. They said that I deserved all of the torture and pain because I was the person who caused this man not to be able to walk. I was having detailed memories of all of the satanic rituals beginning to surface. The pastor's face was all I saw. This was because they continued to do all rituals with pictures of his face posted in front of me. The constant threats were that if he wasn't who I saw that was doing the abuse, then they would leave me all alone. As I have said, this was my biggest fear, because of being tortured since infancy to think that I was evil.

The psychiatrist assigned to me flew out to Colorado to reprogram my core. There was a "pseudo" counseling called rebirthing or holding therapy in Colorado where they wrapped you in a blanket, held you down, and supposedly rebonded with you. This had been used in rituals, and they were experimenting with denial programming to use this to reattach with my programmers through torture. This caused the core to submit to their control and to push the anger of what they did to me down. They wrapped me tightly in blankets and repeatedly kissed me on the cheek. This meant that I was a Judas.

I was a betrayer if I told anybody the truth about what happened. They said that I had sexual feelings while they were kissing me on the cheek, so this proved that they needed to control me. Being held down, kissed over and over, letting water drip on my face while they cuss and threaten me caused intense rage. They said that I was evil because at the core of my being was a raging evil monster. I was afraid of myself, so I pushed all of that rage down and accepted the demons of denial, that they were good loving parents.

There were corporate rituals done while I was in Colorado, as well. They have many underground military ritual sites in the Colorado mountains. A billionaire, Illuminati leader that is in the news a lot recently and is an ANTIFA funder; funds testing on cloning and artificial intelligence in these areas. He is connected to many previous American presidents. The money of the elite goes to buying the presidency and their agenda in this country. This Illuminati leader has set up cloning research labs that are connected to NASA and the military. This council of the elite have set up Facebook as a ploy to set up this nation. Facebook is used to track billions of people, what they do, where they go, who they talk to, every tiny detail of their life. Facebook has been used for sharing the truth of the gospel, praying for people, funding worthy causes, and much more; so it's not at all the root of the evil. The people who control Facebook are the problem. They are trying to take away our freedoms and liberties without us being aware. It is being used as an avenue to track people and know their exact location at all times. The people who control and monitor Facebook have the ability to send electrical waves to affect the communication in the spirit realm. Demonic forces are sent through the air waves and affect our minds. As I sit here trying to write, I'm in a battle. The devil does not want me to get the truth out to people. I refuse to submit to the fear that the evil people are throwing at me daily. They track my e-mail, my phone, and everywhere I go. I have been harassed continually by them since I got free. They have investigators who know where I'm at 24/7, and they send demonic attacks against me continually. I refuse to back down, though. I have been repeatedly given a mandate from Papa God to share the truth of what happened to me so that other people will be set free. Also, so that people will be aware of how the evil people attack and how to fight them. You may not see the effect of their work now, but they are planning and plotting behind the scenes to bring you down and to take away all of your freedom.

Chapter 12

Their Threats

"For those who are evil will be destroyed, but those who hope in the LORD will inherit the land." Psalms 37:9

I was used as a human shield from conception to protect the evil people from being exposed. They worked continually to put in place lie after lie to make me responsible for them. A particular ritual that was detailed and extensive was meant to remind me continually that if I ever exposed the Illuminati, they would torture my brothers. They hooked up my brothers to electrodes and began to electrocute them. As they were doing this, my brothers were screaming nonstop for me to rescue them. I was ripped inside with despair because I couldn't help them. There were loud speakers in the room, and the evil people said that God was speaking through the loud speakers. He said that I was going to hell because I wasn't rescuing my brothers. God said that I was evil and that my programmers couldn't rescue them, because He wasn't going to rescue them. God wanted to expose me as evil. The programmers were in a room, and they had electrodes on them. They began to flop around and act like they were being tortured, because they told me to flip the switch to save my brothers. Then they began to laugh and say they tricked me. I genuinely thought that they were being tortured and that I was saving my brothers, but they said, "See, you're always trying to destroy us." "Honor your father and mother, and you shall have long life." They would quote this over and over. They said since I didn't honor them, I wouldn't have long life, and I would go to hell. Then they brought a man dressed up like Jesus into the room. They made me put electrodes on him and flip the switch. He pretended to be shocked; then he laughed. I heard what I thought was God over the loud speaker continually telling me that I was evil and that I was going to hell. I told the programmer who was pretending to be Jesus that I hated him and I didn't want him because he was torturing me and my brothers. During my ministry time after being set free, Honest Jesus showed me that He hadn't rejected me, and that He was not mad at me. He understood why I didn't want that man and that He wasn't like the evil people. Papa God understood my anger toward Him because I had been so tortured around Him. As the ritual went on, they brought in a man dressed as the devil. He took my programmers into another room. Then I heard horrible excruciating screams that I thought were my programmers. I thought it was my fault that they went to hell and were being tortured, because I had not been good enough it forced God to judge them. At that time, they took me and put me on the "council." They said if I "honored my father and mother," I would always be good. I sat on a council that condemned all people to death; they were burned alive in front of me. I had no way out. I thought I was getting to stop doing evil by sitting on the council and "honoring my father and mother," but it was just another trick.

There is a demonic baton that is passed from the Illuminati leader I was speaking about earlier to each of the programmers. The baton is passed through the electrical system, through TV, phones, radios, and computers. There are grid systems in place with each survivor, electrical implants put in their skin. This allows them to be tracked continually and electrical impulses pushed through their bodies to trigger what they are programmed to do. The grid systems are also connected to all financial systems of wealth. This grid system allows the evil people to send demonic spirits to steal all financial provision from Christians who don't take their authority over what Papa God has given them. When the programmers implant the electrodes into the victim's skin, they take DNA from each of the victims at the same time. They do a ritual where they call in territorial spirits of the past and present and insert the DNA within a robot. Then all victims are told they are a robot. So from our movement to our speech, we believe we are a robot, and we are trained to act like a robot. Then during corporate rituals, the robots that Illuminati are building are called to life with the demonic DNA. The demons wrap around the DNA, and cause a counterfeit of humanity. This is showing up in our culture today, in the life-like sex robots, just do a quick google search. Another example is the robot Sophia that has just been given citizenship by Saudi Arabia. These type of clones and robots have been around for a while. The Illuminati has just been in the process of desensitizing people so that they can bring them into our everyday life. Satan and his children try to pervert and twist all of Papa God's pure creations. There are biologists, chemists, scientists working around the clock to pervert Papa God's creations. Literally, taking the faces off human beings and trying to get them to adhere to the robot. Victims are tormented deliberately to be constantly afraid that there will be a robot out there that looks like them that ends up doing evil things. Then they will be blamed for the evil that happens. Artificial intelligence has been around a long time. They are now just beginning to share some of what they are doing behind the scenes. The reason they are now starting to share some of their evil is they have so desensitized people through TV, movies, and video games to believe that all of this is harmless and pretend. There is insidious evil behind all artificial intelligence and cloning. The military has been infiltrated with the Illuminati elite who have poured billions of dollars into creating robots that are programmed to destroy at the time the evil people activate them. This is called the black awakening.

The man who was forced to pose as my older brother was sent to North Carolina. I began to remember things that they made him do to me. It wasn't his fault. He was being forced to have sex with me and hurt me. The programmers told him that I hated and blamed him. They did not want anything else to surface, so they sent him away. I was distraught that they were going to kill him because of me. The programmers said, "That's what happens when you tell. You're going to end up alone. You're evil." North Carolina was supposed to be the state you went to when you got "perfect enough." There is a *Wizard of Oz* park. They took me to North Carolina and showed me what would happen if I ever told people about them. They gruesomely tortured a person by removing a person's face and placing it on another person, and they forced me to watch the movie *Face Off* to pretend like it didn't happen. They created intense fear and confusion by saying repeatedly, "How did I know who anybody was?" They said that they had switched everybody's face. So I could say someone had done bad things to me, and really they didn't. I would never know who they really are. They told me that they would replace my face with someone else's, and then no person would know where I was and what I was doing. I would be alone and would go crazy. Then they would put me back in the hospital. I was terrified every moment of every day. We stayed in a hotel in North Carolina, and the programming was continually breaking down. I screamed when they were hurting me. A police officer went to our room and asked if there was anybody screaming. They said no, and the police officer left. The police officer assumed that things were fine because we looked like a normal family.

I was forced to start giving a fake "testimony" by speaking at different events that were infiltrated by programmers. Some of the events were at churches that had Illuminati posing as pastors, and the Gideon's. I was forced to say that the pastor they were framing ritualized and raped me. I was made to use the scripture Psalm 18 and Psalm 40. Psalm 40:2 says, "He lifted me out of the slimy pit, out of the mud and mire." My programmers used to keep me in a deep water well beside the house, and they said I should be grateful to them because they got me out of there. If I refused to say that the pastor abused me, they would put me back in the well by myself. I hated being alone in that well. There were rats that I knew could eat people, because I had seen that happen. There were insects that crawled all over me. I was living a horror story, and I didn't see any way out. So I told people that the pastor had abused me, not them. I was not consciously doing this. All the different parts of my mind had blocked things completely out of my memory. The other scripture they made me quote was Psalm 18, which says, "The Lord is my rock, my fortress and my deliverer; my God is my rock, in whom I take refuge, my shield, and the horn of my salvation, my stronghold. I called to the Lord, who is worthy of praise, and I have been saved from my enemies. The cords of death entangled me; the torrents of destruction overwhelmed me. The cords of the grave coiled around me; the snares of death confronted me. In my distress I called to the Lord; I cried to my God for help. From his temple, he heard my voice." The evil people took ropes and tied them around my neck and said that since he (the male programmer) was God, I had to cry out to him to rescue me. I was told that if I ever told anybody about what they had done to me, they would send me back to the hospital. They would remind me over and over they were protecting people from me, so I should be grateful to them.

I was truly gifted from Papa God with the gift of speaking. The programmers used this genuine gift from Papa God as leverage to keep me bound with them. I was in too deep they said, and nobody would ever believe me after I gave the testimony that the pastor had done the abuse. There were programmers at each place I spoke to intimidate me. They were there to see the programming in action. They were also there to program me more so that I would never expose them. This was so confusing, because I genuinely loved my speaking ability. I thought that I really must like being evil, and I hated myself more for having a gift in speaking. Down at the core of my being in the unconscious mind, I knew that the pastor was innocent and my programmers were getting away with hideous evil. I had no idea how to get free; I was trapped. I had been told over an over that I was stupid, dumb, and that I wasn't good at anything except sex. According to everything I had been told, I was only good at sex, because God had made me to have sex and didn't give me anything else as a gift. My mind was so confused; I felt guilty and evil every second of every day.

The evil people see all the gifts that are spiritually given to the victims by Papa God, and they pervert those on purpose. The reason they do this is the gift is powerful in showing victims their identity in Papa God. The enemy fights hard to destroy and pervert all gifts and talent given to us by Papa God. For example, I was able to put clothes together fashionably in a very artistic way. The programmers took a victim and cut them up in pieces. They said that that's why I had that gift; then I had to put all of the pieces of the people back together. So every time that I had to put an outfit together for the people I was sold to, I thought of that, and I felt evil for having that gift. I thought all gifts were evil. I was told over and over, "You can only be good at what we say you can be good at, because you use everything for evil." After my rescue, during my healing, Papa God showed me as I was getting dressed one day how He put a beautiful outfit together for me to wear, down to every detail. He was showing me that He created that gift, and it was not evil. He shared that He is creative, and, therefore, we are creative. He has a beautiful detailed woven plan for each of us, even if we can't see the plan.

Around this time, I was taken to a Benny Hinn conference in New York by the female programmer. New York is considered the final destination for victims. It is where the biggest corporate Illuminati rituals are done. They gather all of the victims together to get them linked corporately. New York stands for slavery for victims. The Illuminati torture and train us to believe it stands for the freedom for victims. New York is where we are forced to start Illuminati war on the US and take down the Christians. Each of us has been trained as mind-controlled soldiers, and do a job that we have been programmed to do at the end. The battle is really for our minds. If they can control our minds, they will be in control of all of what we do. These jobs are the only way we are told we can earn freedom. Killing a Christian for us means our bloodline will be transformed to a pure bloodline. This destroys the curse that God put on us and gives us the ability to be pure. The poem that represents the Statue of Liberty was used in the rituals. *Give me your tired, your poor. Your huddled masses yearning to breathe free. The wretched refuse of your teeming shore. Send these, the homeless, tempest-tossed to me, I lift my lamp beside the golden door!* If we allowed the Illuminati to own us, then we could earn our freedom. They told us that in the end there will be bombings at all of the landmarks in New York, and there will be concentration camps set up. There were programmers at the conference; they recorded all of the preaching and used them in the rituals. They dressed up to look like the speakers and tortured me and many other victims to keep us from believing what the preachers were saying.

The Illuminati is constantly targeting ministries. They had a list of ministries that minister to Satanic ritual abuse survivors that they wanted to bring down. They send victims to these ministries to discredit them and destroy the ministry against their wills. They take at least a year and begin to program us to destroy the ministry. My programmers targeted a ministry that was working with SRA victims and getting some results. They got all of the Christian ministry's music, teaching materials, pictures, and all their friends and ministry partners names, and sent demons to scan them. This means that the demons find out about all of their weaknesses, wounds, and issues, and relay them back to the Illuminati. I began being tortured and programmed around them a year before they sent me there. They also sent three other victims at the same time so they could pit us against each other. They ritualized all of us together to make sure that we were programmed against each other sufficiently. Also, to make sure we didn't trust each other. Each of us were sent with the agenda to take down the ministry. We did not go there consciously knowing why were sent there; we were completely disassociated. I was told that the ministry couple was going to be taking over as my programmers. So even though they were loving and kind to me, I just thought that was an act. The evil people sent me under the disguise that they were a perfect loving family trying to get their daughter the healing she needed. After twenty-five years of torture and rape, never having anything else, I thought that this was all that would ever happen to me. They told me if I went there and worked for seven years, I would be allowed to get married. If I got married, I could genuinely be free, because the man who was my husband would be my controller, and I wouldn't have to keep being tortured. This was all a lie, of course. But I believed that this was my only way out and the only way I would be chosen.

Chapter 13

A Setup

"In his arrogance the wicked man hunts down the weak, who are
caught in the schemes he devises. He boasts about the cravings
of his heart; he blesses the greedy and reviles the LORD. In his
pride the wicked man does not seek him; in all his thoughts there
is no room for God. His ways are always prosperous; your laws are
rejected by him; he sneers at all his enemies. He says to himself,
"Nothing will ever shake me." He swears, "No one will ever do me
harm." His mouth is full of lies and threats; trouble and evil are
under his tongue. He lies in wait near the villages; from ambush he
murders the innocent. His eyes watch in secret for his victims; like a
lion in cover he lies in wait. He lies in wait to catch the helpless; he
catches the helpless and drags them off in his net." Psalms 10:2-10

As I began to get ministry from this couple, I began to remember
specific details of what happened to me. They never asked me any
questions about the abuse or told me what they thought happened.
They just asked Papa God to heal me and show me the truth. I didn't
remember the programmers' faces, but the genuine Holy Spirit kept
revealing memories, and each time I got healing, I started to see the
faces clearer. There were parts that were seeing the truth and parts
that were still in denial, so I kept getting tortured and raped by the
programmers during this time. It's difficult for people to understand
why I kept going back. The reality is that after twenty-five years of

the type of torture I went through, I didn't have any idea that there was anything different. I had been deliberately divided in my mind by the programmers. I had thousands of parts within my mind that were still trying to get free and see the truth. So day by day, I would get truth from Papa God, and I would continue to be ritualized by the evil people. I had no idea that I could actually be free, or *that* anybody would want me to be free. I dearly loved this couple and their children, but I didn't trust them. I had been tortured and programmed about every detail of their life. I was being lied to about every single thing about them and what they did. They had set up people around this couple who were programmers as well. There was a church that was led by a victim, and there was a covenant and pact made to keep all of the victims quiet about what was planned. There were victims on the worship team, and there was a programmer on the worship team. He would stare at us while we sang. He was involved in all of the military programming and the Jewish programming. He would do all of the torture to cover up and distort the core as much as possible the core knew who he was. When I mention the core, I'm talking about the part of my being that knew everything—all of the torture, rape, and abuse I went through. The main objective of the programmer was to bury the core. This included the monarch programming that was done in underground tunnels, and it was the deepest level of programming. They never wanted this information to be recovered. They tried to bury the core by making us so terrified of ourselves that we would never allow those memories to surface. There was a Judas program to keep us from ever telling the truth about what we were going through; if we did, we would be Judas. This meant that we would be responsible for the death and torture of the other victims. The programmer in the church raped us and would take us out to eat after church. The food we ate were used in the rituals. The cheese sauce was used as a representative of the ejaculation. And this reminded us that we were whores. He had cameras all over his house. His wife was a victim. He was connected to all of the German military programmers. He had a daughter who was tortured with me and that they put a competition between us. They switched our children and made us earn them back. If I pretended like the programmer wasn't evil, I would get my children back.

There was a corporate ritual done on the day we were all sent to Kentucky to take down the ministry. It was done on the night of the conference that the Christian couple was leading. The programmers for all the women were sent there and were involved in the ritual. My programmer was at the conference, and she stayed there when I was getting ministry from the couple. Programmers who were posing as ministers from Neil Anderson's Freedom in Christ were also there to destroy this ministry. Every time I got ministry from the innocent Christian couple, I was tortured around them and around the way that they did ministry. I was told that the couple was trying to get to the core of who I was, to expose how evil I was. The evil people told me that their ministry was to reveal all of the evil I did so that people would know about it. Reality was that they were asking the genuine Holy Spirit to reveal the lies I believed and to bring truth. I was told lies about every aspect of the ministry that was just trying to help me.

The programmers' main strategy was to force me to say they were perfect, and if I did not say they were perfect I would be exposed as evil. They were continually playing games with my mind. The Christian couple innocently watched a movie called *The Game*, and recommended I watch it. They did not know that I had been tortured to believe that my life was a game. In this movie, just like the movie *The Truman Show*, everybody knew what was going on but the main character. The main objective like the programming I went through was to manipulate and confuse to the point they would not be able to discern between reality and the game.

There was another lady who was doing the same type of ministry that was genuinely trying to help me. She was friends with the Christian couple. My programmer took me to many ministry sessions with her, and then I ended up living with her and her family. My programmers targeted her and her family. I loved this family very much, but I was tortured to believe they were setting me up too. They sent jealousy demons to cause conflict in the house between her daughters and me. I thought I was the "evil one." The programmers told me that I was the mixed breed in their house. They put poison in the dog's food, and he got really sick. The female programmer brought brownies that had metal in them, and they made the Christian lady get sick. I was too terrified to allow the truth to start to surface, because my programmers said that they would kill these people and then say I did it. I was still getting tortured and raped by my programmers while I stayed at this family's house. I would go for walks on their large property and have to meet the programmers. I would get raped to remind me that I was not allowed to talk about anything other than what they told me I could. There were denial parts of my mind that were functioning for me. I had no memory of what was going on in the present. I had many religious programs working. I would read the Bible all the time, because if I read the Bible, it would remind me of how evil I was. The programmers told me the "sons of Belial" in the Bible refers to me. I ended up moving out of their house because I was still in major denial about my programmers and ended up in an apartment. There was a victim, a man who was assigned to me with a name that resembled "demon," and he had been friends with that family for many years. He was with me all the time, and the evil people ritualized us together to bury the truth about my programmers.

I kept getting ministry, and Papa God kept bringing deeper memories. My memories were never coerced or implied by anyone; all of my memories were brought out by the Holy Spirit. Finally, the denial wall broke in some of my parts, and I was able to see all of the memories and who they were linked to, and some of my parts began seeing who my programmers really were. I was put in a job as a gymnastics instructor with another victim. We were tortured in the gymnastics building. It was a large old building with an upstairs, so there was a lot of room, and noise could not be heard easily. Papa God began bringing back memories of what happened in the gymnastics job, so I quit that. I then moved in with the Christian couple. They gave me a place to live, a job, a car, and food. They prayed for me and ministered to me on a regular basis. Other programmers were put in place all around this couple to bring them down. They had no idea what was going on. The other victims that were sent to take down the ministry were there too. There was still great torment and confusion in my mind unconsciously of whether the Christian couple were evil like my programmers had tortured me to believe. I continued to get ritualized at night by coded messages or through the programmers they set up in that town. I would get a phone call or a sign or symbol in front of me to make me go to the rituals. I still was unconscious of the rituals that were going on and of the fact that I was still under my programmers control.

I moved into a house with a girl who was sent with me to destroy the ministry. This was planned, because the Illuminati had programmed us against each other severely. She was very harsh, angry, and mean on the outside. And I was the person who was kind, quiet, and timid on the outside. In the rituals, she was timid and quiet, and I was the angry, mean person. My part that was trained to be an animal was out in the rituals. I had to growl and intimidate, or people would be killed. She had to be quiet and timid. They told each of us that it was our fault the other person got tortured. So we didn't trust each other in any way. We kept the programs and systems going to protect ourselves and other people. When we looked at each other, we saw what we hated about ourselves. It was a constant reminder. Then our programmers brought a man whom we had to share to this town. I was going to be allowed to marry the man in the natural, and she was allowed to marry him in the ritual life. This made our hate and competition even greater. He was our "Jacob," and we took turns being Leah and Rachel. If we followed through with the plan against the Christian couple, we would get the man; that would give us freedom all the time, and he would be our husband. This meant to us that we would not do evil ever again, and we would be controlled. And it also meant that we wouldn't have to be tortured and tormented for the rest of our life.

The Illuminati targeted the children of the people who were ministering to us and sent victims to be married to their children. This way, they could control their ability to expose the truth about them. There were victims and programmers who were placed around the Christian couple within their church so that I would go to their homes and be ritualized, but the Christian couple wouldn't have any idea. I just thought this was normal and that everybody was involved in torturing me. I thought that the Christian couple were my new programmers and that they had set up for me to go to be programmed somewhere else. But the reality was that they had no idea what was really going on.

I was put in a job as a case manager at a company, and the girl I was living with was put in a job as a support specialist who took the kids to outings at the same company. This was another setup by the Illuminati. We had to go into homes and spend time with children. Specific child victims were chosen; the evil people took pictures raping us and forcing us to have to do sexual things with the children. We had no choice, but the programmers said it was our fault, and they said that they would take the pictures to police and put us away forever if we told anybody. There were already police who were involved with the rituals. There was also a judge who was a programmer. We were terrified to tell anybody. They would make us bond with the children and teenagers and then force us to hurt them, and we had no way out. In the job I was put in, I had to put children into hospitals if the judge (programmer) ordered it. Then I would have to visit the hospital and get ritualized with the children. There was a hospital in Kentucky that had a whole room just dedicated to *Wizard of Oz* programming.

No matter how much the Christian couple gave me, I still couldn't see that I was loved. They gave me Christmas presents, birthday presents, and holidays; took us on trips; and took me out to eat. They shared their family time with me and spent countless hours of ministry with me. Their children were so kind to me and gave me kind notes and played like little kids with me. I had been trained that if people didn't say they were my father and mother, then that meant they were against me, and wanted me to be a mixed breed. This meant to me that they were not willing to share their pure bloodline. The evil people used this to cause me to never let the unconscious into the conscious—for the parts of my mind that knew the truth to stay hidden.

The "Jacob" victim whom the programmers sent for the final plan against this ministry had just recently gotten out of jail (where he was being tortured). He was sent to where I was to be my new handler and cult chosen husband. I was given a ring that was a "princess" cut for the perfect princess programming. He asked me to marry him by the river next to the bridge. This meant that he was the bridge to freedom for me. He and his sister were victims, and their father had married a victim twice. Their dad had no idea that his children were victims. He was involved in doing Christian ministry also, and he ministered to me some. This was confusing, because the evil people had tortured me around him. The evil people said that he was working to expose that I wasn't good enough for his son. They would electrocute me over and over and say, "What did you do?" So when I would be in a ministry session and he would ask, "What did you do?" I thought he was saying that I was evil. I would shut down and not allow healing to happen.

Chapter 14

Journey to Freedom

"I believe that in the end the truth will conquer." John Wycliffe

At this point in my story, I'm going to walk you through step by step on how I got free—starting with the time I faced the people who set me up and who had tried to make me to destroy the Christian couple.

While walking into the police department, meeting face-to-face with people who wanted to destroy me and the people I cared about, I felt terror—terror for what they might do to me, and even more for what they might make me do.

I was afraid of going into the denial programming, with all of the past thirty-one years of being brainwashed, afraid that the mind control would be too strong and I would be tricked again. The unconscious was flooding through into the conscious, and it was excruciating, but it was freeing at the same time. I see the kindness of Papa God in giving us the ability to block out certain things that are too traumatic for our minds. Unfortunately, the evil people had deliberately used that defense mechanism intended to shield us from traumatic events, as a curse that was used against me to keep me in bondage to them. They deliberately forced my mind to forget and break off into pieces to endure the pain that they inflicted.

Every day since I had escaped and ran to get away from the evil people till today, I had spent day after day screaming, crying, and praying in my car for Papa God to show me the truth and rescue my mind from the hold that they had on me. Memory after memory had been flooding back, and with it was intense emotion.

On the way to the police department, I was searching my mind of anything that would be triggered and cause me to be under their control. I was afraid they would access some part of my mind that was not yet free from their control. I had gotten so much freedom in my mind over the seven years of ministry I had received from the Christian couple, and then God gave me a window of opportunity to get physically free.

Standing in the presence of my enemies, I was afraid, but most of all, I felt peace knowing that I was doing the most loving thing I could do. I was laying down my life to protect my friends. "Greater love has no one than this: to lay down one's life for one's friends" (John 15:13).

Papa God had it all planned in a way that this day is my last day in the *40 Days of Purpose* book I was reading. Just like when the Israelites walked out of Egypt, in the midst of the Egyptians, I was walking out of slavery in the midst of my abusers and captors. It reminded me of the scripture "And Elisha prayed, 'Open his eyes, LORD, so that he may see.' Then the LORD opened the servant's eyes, and he looked and saw the hills full of horses and chariots of fire all around Elisha" (2 Kings 6:17). The minister and friend I was now laying my life down for reminded me that with God my adversaries are nothing before me. Papa God and I outnumbered them!

The detective who had participated in the satanic rituals and abuse was there, and he took my phone from me. He was checking to see if there was any recording device on me. He had a lot to lose, so he couldn't have me taping anything that could incriminate him.

I went into a room with two people, a detective, and a police officer, each who had raped, tortured, and abused me. Even the judge in this town was one of my abusers. They were doing everything they could do to trick, control, manipulate, and cause me to break. They kept questioning me, trying to get me to go into the satanic ritual part of the abuse so they could discredit me and try to make me to look crazy. Papa God gave me insight, so I would not fall for their tricks.

The cards were stacked completely against me, but something reverberated inside my being: with Papa God, I was the majority. I didn't care if I was going to get into trouble or if I was going to be hurt, I just knew I had to tell the truth. I had determined in my heart that I would tell the truth no matter the consequences. So I testified to the truth of what my programmers had done to me—that he had raped me, as he had every day of my life. I told this to the police officer and detective who were involved in the entire setup. This was the last thing they expected me to say; they thought I was going to follow the plan. The hold they once had on my mind wasn't there anymore. Without the mind control, they could not do anything to me.

They were trying to torment me to make me terrified that I would be put in jail for not saying what they wanted me to say. Jail represented hell to me, I had been put in many cages, and I knew what could happen if they put me there. I had already had the rape kit completed on me, with the same police officer in the room who was interrogating me. I said the same thing the day when the rape testing had been done—that the evil people raped me. The police officer was pretending like I had never stated that truth, that the programmer had raped me. I plainly stated that he had raped me, and I did not waver in anyway.

There was false evidence as well. There was DNA that pointed to the Christian minister who had rescued me as the criminal. That was the part of the plan that I did follow through with. I got the DNA from the Christian couple's house, and I took it to the evil people. I couldn't bear the thought of what they had told me would happen if I didn't follow through with their plan. I would be alone, and all of the evil in me would be available for everyone to see. I would kill people and torture people all the time, for all eternity. And there would be no one there to control me, no one there to keep me from being evil.

I had been trained all my life that I would get a husband who would be with me every second and would keep me from being evil. That was my only way out of all of this. If I didn't follow through with their plan, I wouldn't get to marry him, and I would lose what I thought was the only way out. If I didn't follow through with getting the evidence, I would have to hurt the Christian couple's children. I could not bear the thought of that. Even death was not an option they said. Death for me was not an option, because I never would die. I had been programmed over and over that I would just keep doing the evil things they trained me to do, so that is why I never got around to killing myself.

People ask me why I didn't kill myself during all of this; the cult ensures that we do not kill ourselves. They make death seem like an option that is even worse than living. They set up rooms that they torture us in and called it hell, and told us what happens to people who kill themselves.

The plan for seven years had been that I was sent to this ministry by the evil people to destroy and take down the ministry and people who ran the ministry. They prepared me long before I was sent there. When the seven years of work was over that the evil people sent us there for. They got the book the couple had written, their training manual, and did rituals around the material in the book. They took the couple's picture, forced me to look at it, and raped me while saying that the couple had told them to do it. They played their music while they were torturing me. They demanded that we say the man who genuinely ministered to us and had done so much for us had raped us. Still at this point, we were still in denial, and not consciously aware of what we were doing. I had no idea in the conscious realm that I was trying to set up a man. After being tortured beyond what is humanly imaginable and threatened to be forced to molest his children in order for them to stay alive, I went to the Christian couple's house and got a pair of underwear to get DNA from the man. I gave the underwear to the Illuminati, and was in the fight of my life. I was put in a room with the detective, my programmers, the judge, and the police who were involved. They brought out every picture that they had taken of me and said that I would be sent to jail where I would have no person to control me. I would be forced to kill, torture, and molest children, including their children, for the rest of my life. I was still under the programmers' mind control. I told the Christian couple's family member I was raped by the programmer, and then the police who was involved showed up to do a rape kit. They did a rape kit. I told them specifically that my programmer raped me. But they did not allow that to be written down. I had finally gotten a revelation of what genuine love is. I wasn't rejected by the Christian couple after all I had been forced to do. They genuinely accepted me still. That did something huge in my system. I had never in my life been accepted, and especially if I had made a mistake. I had to be perfect every second; and even when I performed perfectly, I was tortured, raped, and rejected. This couple did not reject me even after the horrible mistake I made. That broke a huge denial wound in my life, and all of the memories started flooding in. I got by myself and screamed and cried and let all of the memories flood in. I chose to tell the truth. The programmers had raped me every day of my life, and the Christian man never raped me, not ever! At this point, I knew I had to get away from all of the evil that had been set up to destroy me in that town. The girl I lived with was still going to rituals, and she was with the programmers. So I had to get out of there. I asked Papa God where to go, and He showed me a place. I moved by myself without telling anybody where I was going. I didn't speak to anybody, because I was so afraid of being tricked. I spent all of my time in my car screaming and looking at all of the memories that kept surfacing. I was tormented that maybe I was doing evil or that maybe I wasn't conscious that I was still going back to my programmers. I was in terror constantly. This is what the evil people controlled me with—fear and terror—constantly. I had no idea how to do things, like go grocery shopping. When I went anywhere, I was always looking around wondering who was watching me and when they would show up and destroy me. The truth now was that I was not controlled anymore in my mind, so they had no way to get to me any longer. It was so horribly difficult to believe that I was free. I had always believed there was no way out of the horror that I endured. Another way they tortured me for decades was to make me think I was never aware of anything that I did from minute to minute. So this fear was a huge mountain to climb. But day by day, memory by memory, I stepped further into healing. A song that meant so much to me while I was going through all of that was "Voice of Truth," by Casting Crowns. He was the Voice of Truth, after all of the lies I had been told every second, of every day, for all of my life. His Voice of Truth was winning, and I was getting free in my mind! Another thing I held onto at that time was a poem given to me by the Christian couple who helped me get free. It was by Roy Lessin: "Just think you're here not by chance, but by God's choosing. His Hand formed you and made you the person you are. He compares you to no one else-you are one of a kind. You lack nothing that His grace can't give you. He has allowed you to be here, at this time in history, to fulfill His special purpose for this generation."

The evil people told me that the Christian couple were going to take over programming and controlling me. They had used the movie *Truman Show* as a torture ritual movie, saying that the couple they were sending me to were going to be the people who were in the control tower in the movie. They would be controlling every detail of my life now according to my programmers. If you watch this movie, it is a mind-control movie. He lives a fake life, and everybody around him are in on it, except he is unaware of what is really going on. I just thought that these were my new "controllers," the new people who would train me to be good enough. This had happened many times before, so I didn't think this would be any different.

The evil people targeted this ministry because the ministry was making significant headway with rescuing people from satanic ritual abuse. The people who ran that ministry had only been loving and kind to me; they never hurt me. They had ministered to me, given me a place to live, a car, a job, and food to eat. I had never been loved or cared for by anyone in my life, so they were gradually bit by bit crumbling the wall that the evil people had put up inside my mind.

The Illuminati officials said they had already talked to the other victims, making me think they had given them information about the Christian couple. The police officer knew where I lived now. She knew I had just gotten a job. They had been watching me. I had been so scared that I had not gone out of the house or been around people unless I absolutely had to because of work.

They were trying to intimidate me. But I knew the setup, and I showed them I would not be their slave any longer. I told them the truth that I had gotten the DNA from the couple's house, and I had planted it so that he would be made responsible for the rape. They were pushing me to talk to reveal something that would give them something to destroy me with, so they could try and make me sound crazy in case I tried to expose them.

Just like Psalms 57:6 says, "They spread a net for my feet—I was bowed down in distress. They dug a pit in my path—but they have fallen into it themselves." They could not trap me this time. I would not go there with them. I would not fall for their traps. Papa God was with me, and He was giving me insight and strength.

I told the police officer and the detective I was afraid of the real person who had raped me, the programmer. He raped me, and he was the person, as well as the female programmer, who had abused and tortured me all these years. Even today, I want to deny the truth that I could go through with something so heinous and hurtful. That I would be willing to take a person's DNA and destroy them with it is unconscionable, especially a person who had only given me love and the possibility of genuine life.

I have no excuses that are valid. I only have the reality of the thirty years of the fear, torture, and torment of the evil people that drove me to it. I only wanted to be a decent person, and the irony was that when I finally admitted to the most hideous thing I had ever done, is when I finally saw that I wasn't evil at all. I was free and capable of standing up for truth even in the face of a death sentence.

I was not a hero. I am a flawed human being in need of a Savior. He rescued me. The same Savior still rescues me every day from my horrible memories. As I write this, many emotions, pain, and hurt surfaces; but I choose to focus on how Papa God is going to use this book to rescue many people, and raise up an army of people who will fight to set the captives free.

Each of us are born with a gift of choice, which God gave. On a daily basis, we can decide whether to choose Jesus or not. Millions of people are robbed of choice. They are enslaved and are given no choices. I was thirty-one years old when finally, for the first time ever,

I was given a choice, and I had finally experienced genuine unconditional love. I was free. The ministry couple did not reject me, even
after knowing all of the plans of the evil people that I had gone there
with to destroy them. They chose to love me and see that I was doing
the very best I could at that time. When they forgave me, I was
changed. I made a decision to tell the truth no matter what.

I could be free. Jesus wanted me free. Even after all I had done,
this couple wanted me to be free. So I told the truth. I told the truth
even though I was petrified of myself and of what they would do to
me. When Jesus "passes by," we can let him pass by. Or we can reach
out and take the healing He has to offer us. Sometimes, this will be
excruciatingly painful, but the pain will be worth it. Because if we
don't reach out, we will live in a world of denial, lies, and continual
pain for the rest of our lives. At the end of John 8, it is written that
the Jews rejected the truth about Jesus being the Son of God. As the
Jews took up stones to throw at Jesus, "Jesus hid Himself and went
out of the temple, going through the midst of them, and so 'passed
by.'" The Jews missed out on getting to know Jesus in a special way.
He was their opportunity for freedom. He is still holding out His
hand to and bringing the Jews to Himself, His chosen people. His
promises will be fulfilled to them.

Chapter 15

Set Free

"Now the Lord is the Spirit, and where the Spirit of
the Lord is, there is freedom." 2 Corinthians 3:17

Jesus passed by the evil people at a point in their life. They knew
the Bible. They knew who Jesus was. Yet they willfully chose to reject
Jesus. They chose power, money, pride, and evil instead. They gave
their entire beings over to Satan, and there was no limit to the evil
they were capable of. They had asked the demons to indwell and live
within them and for Satan to take their body and use it however he
wanted to.

In John 9, Jesus "passed by" a man who was blind since birth.
The man chose to allow Jesus to heal him, and he had a personal
experience of healing and freedom with Jesus. The Pharisees chose
not to believe in Jesus. Papa God showed me that He was and still
is all about choices. He would never force anybody to follow Him.
Even salvation is a choice. He will not force anybody to go to heaven.
He is not an evil God who sends people to hell. He is a kind God
who gives every single person a choice on whether they want to go to
heaven or not. He is the Way, the Truth, and the Life.

I continue to get more and more insights from John 8 and 9.
I thought I was through with all of the revelation I could get from
this, but then Papa God said, "Go back there." This shows me the
immense amount of treasures in the Word. I always was tortured to

read the Bible, because they said it was written to make me remember how evil I was. The Bible for victims is like the electric chair, because of the torture we endured every time when it was read. The scriptures were read at the rituals and twisted to mean whatever they wanted them to mean. It was just like when Satan used the scripture to tempt and torment Jesus in the wilderness. If condemnation and shame are felt and a wrong image of Jesus is given by the Scripture, it is not the Spirit of God that is unfolding before for us.

If you look at John 9, for example, and you put all of the emphasis on us to make right choices to "see" Jesus as He passes by, we miss the reality that it says, "He saw us first." He did not only see us in the physical realm; He also saw our pain, our hurt, our deepest feelings. He has felt what we felt, because He was there, and He saw all that we experienced and experienced it with us. Jesus experienced the pain and the shame that the blind man felt when people judged him. The people said that the blind man did something to cause the blindness that he was born with. Jesus sincerely wanted to take the blindness away. Jesus wanted to take the sting of the rejection the blind man felt as people judged and labeled him. Jesus cares, and He wants to heal us. Today, as I listened to the pastor speak at church, he was talking about Jesus "passing by" the woman with the issue of blood. Luke 8:40–48 says, "Jesus was on His way to heal Jairus daughter. When the crowd 'pressed in' to get to Jesus." Jesus is a gentleman. He will not force anybody to have a relationship with Him, but He gives us opportunity after opportunity to press in and see His face and His healing. The reason He wants us to press in is not so that He will get something. He always genuinely wants to give us something. He is always available to us. He passes by to remind us of that. The lady with the issue of blood knew that she could touch Him and be healed. He didn't even have to touch her. "Then the woman, seeing that she could not go unnoticed, came trembling and fell at his feet. In the presence of all the people, she told why she had touched him and how she had been instantly healed. Then he said to her, 'Daughter, your faith has healed you. Go in peace.'" She testified of her wounds and how Jesus had healed her in the presence of people. Our testimony of what Jesus has done in our life as we partner with him is powerful!

I found a church that the Christian couple knew of and moved there. I genuinely needed a church in this new town. I went to church with terror filling my mind, and I left without speaking to anybody. I ended up going to a Sunday school class with people who were so kind, but I was still so afraid. I was about one hundred pounds. Because I was so afraid all the time, I couldn't eat. I chose to genuinely trust Papa God, and I went to eat with a couple from that church. I took a few bites of food; then I got in my car to go, and I threw up all over the car because of the stress and fear.

I kept making tiny steps to believe that I was free. This battle was for my mind. One layer at a time, I began to get the truth that I needed. I ended up being friends with that couple who took me to lunch and her sister. They were very kind. They provided food through our Sunday school class and helped me find a job. There were so many times that Papa God took care of me! I became so close to the Christian couple and their children, and I missed them so much! I had lost my genuine family, the only thing close to a family that I had ever had. Papa God began bringing people who weren't evil to replace all that I lost. There were so many times I was so lonely, and I cried to Papa God, and then a person would ask me to go eat with them. Then I would keep asking God if the person could be trusted or not. I was terrified of trusting anybody, and I didn't even trust Papa God. Many times, a person at church or Sunday school would give me exactly what I needed to buy my groceries. I had a check show up in the mail that covered my rent. I would not have anything to eat for lunch, and someone at work who didn't know that I was hungry would bring lunch in for me.

Another couple in Sunday school class, asked me to spend time with them. I was so scared of the possibility of the people who tried to approach me, might be evil. That day, the pastor of the church I went attended, spoke about geese and how they fly in a V formation, which is to allow for some other goose to take over when the leader gets tired. Geese can fly 71% percent farther with each other. I genuinely felt this was the Holy Spirit telling me that I needed people.

I went over to the couple's house that day, and geese flew over the house just as I was about to go in. I cried. This was Papa God's sign that I didn't have to be afraid. They took me in as family, and I lived with them for a while. They included me like family. I spent holidays with them and their relatives. She and her sister were big influences in my healing, and we all were growing together in spiritual things. Her little girl asked me one day, "Do you have a mama?" I said no. She had a little battery-powered pink VW Beetle. She said, "Well, I would have picked you up in my VW Beetle, and you could be my family." Amazing how children can say just what Papa God needs us to hear. Children are safe, and they are pure, so He ministers through them often.

This family fed me, prayed for me, and just provided a secure place for me to be. During this time, I was working through memories daily by myself, and a man at work told me about someone who did ministry and moved there from Florida. I remember Papa God showing me a vision of Honest Jesus (I began calling Jesus "Honest Jesus" because He doesn't lie), and Honest Jesus was saying this was the person I had prayed for to minister to me. I prayed for somebody to minister to me because I was dealing with all of this trauma and mind control by myself. When I first met with him and his wife, I saw his face like a demon. The devil and Illuminati did not want me to meet this man. He was doing great work of healing for Papa God. He began to minister to me, and I began to have genuine peace a step at a time. Lie after lie was being destroyed, and truth was being brought. Papa God spoke to this man to be my spiritual papa. I had never had a man who took the role of papa in my life. He was a great example of what having a papa does for your life. There were so many revelations I got from Papa God by having a spiritual papa! Papa God showed me how my papa knew my voice and cry, and could pick me out of a crowd of people. Papa God is like that a million times over! My spiritual papa told me how proud he was of me; that ministered to me greatly!

I got an opportunity to go to India on a mission trip through Truth in Love ministry. I was scared, but I genuinely felt like Papa God was telling me to go. My spiritual papa and a team were going,

TO TELL THE TRUTH

so I felt secure. The finances for the trip poured in! I even had an elderly man pay for my haircut one day after hearing I was going on a mission trip. There was a two-week intensive all-day deliverance class that I would have an opportunity to go through. Before I went, I visited my spiritual papa's mentor and spiritual dad. He didn't speak and was in a nursing home. While I was there, he spoke! He said, "Meet them, greet them, and pray for them." That was my mission in India! Papa God provided all of the money for the trip. On the flight to India, memory after memory of the torture and rape on the flights that the Illuminati put me on started flooding back. When the plane started getting bumpy, I was terrified, because I remembered the things that happened on those flights. When I was little, they told me we were going to crash on the flights. They said this so I would vow to follow the Antichrist so I could raise the people from the dead that were on the plane when we crashed. They tricked me to do this so the Antichrist demons would have a legal right to be there.

When I got to India for our mission trip, I began to cry. I was terrified, and I didn't know why. I began having body memories, and the sights and smells of India began to bring back memory after memory of being taken there and tortured. When we were there, I began to feel movement like coils of a snake inside my stomach, intestines, jaw, hands, and feet. These were serpent spirits that were attacking me. They would coil up in my eyes and look like spirals going around and around, and they would try and take me demonically to different dimensions. Praying in tongues breaks the Morse code of the demons that are attacking people. I prayed a deliverance prayer, and Papa God made the demons go away. We took a train to get to our motel after getting off the plane. I was trafficked and ritualized on the train when I was a kid. They chained all of the children together on the train when I was taken to India as a child. They didn't let us eat, and we had to use the bathroom on ourselves. So I was in severe anxiety and terror as I was reliving this on my mission trip. It was an overnight train, so everyone went to sleep that was on my team. I was so scared I didn't sleep at all. I was miserable. The warfare of the territory was causing intense stomach and body pains. I got an eye infection that made my eyes turn completely blood red. This caused the memories about how I was tortured in India flood back. I was poked in my eyes with needles, and I was starved there. I had insects and rats that crawled all over me. There was a commander who was part of the police force there, and he tortured me and took over my programming. I had lice and scabies, and was treated like a dog.

When I was a child, the main programmers showed up and would dress me up, feed me, and sell me there in India. I was sold in all the different caste systems in India. If I made the programmers money, they would let me take a shower. There was always a price tag on every single basic human need I had. There was a white witch whom they worshiped in India, and she would kill the children and eat them if I didn't do what she said. I just wanted to rescue the children, but I couldn't. They said if I just pretended and got the attention of men, I would be allowed to have clothes. I didn't think I was going to survive this mission trip because of the flooding of memories every day. The love of Papa God was so kind. He brought little children to sit by me in India, and that healed my heart. We were outside during our deliverance and inner healing ministry time while in India. I took stickers and candy for the kids. Most of them had never had those things before. I was able to pray over all of the children. I will never forget that!

While the teaching and deliverance was happening in India, there were bugs everywhere, because the classes were outside at night. I was so angry, and upset because it reminded me of the bugs that the evil people would allow to crawl all over me. They would say, "Don't move. Don't blink. Stand still," while the bugs were crawling all over me and biting me. If I moved, I got in trouble.

During the mission trip, I got major deliverance over all of the territorial demons in India. Papa God cut off the Illuminati serpents' heads and shut the mouth of the lion, the devil. Papa God showed me that this deliverance broke chains off all the other victims as well. Before a deliverance time, there was a beautiful butterfly that flew over top all of the people. The class name was Transformations. Papa God was really transforming lives! By the end of the trip, I had genuinely fallen in love with the people of India. They were so honoring and loving. They sat our team at the front and gave us flowers. I met a lady from India who treated me like a daughter and loved me unconditionally. After my deliverance, she would wash my face from all of the crying, fix my hair, and pat my back. I had never had that before. I ended up going back to India two more times. I was asked to give my testimony in India about how Papa God rescued me. At the end of the deliverance, when we were sharing how we were healed. Honest Jesus showed me He was taking His sword and destroying the evil people and Satan. My spiritual papa was seeing me with a sword doing the same thing with Honest Jesus! It was so healing to share my testimony in a place where I had been tortured and raped as a child.

When I got back from India the last time I went, I gave my testimony at the church I attended here in America. Papa God knew how difficult this was for me because there was a programmer who went to the same church. I was not being accessed any longer, but she and her husband were constantly trying to intimidate me and cause me to be afraid. I had made the pastor aware of the situation, and he listened. Unfortunately, he was not aware of the depth of evil they were capable of. That is one of the reasons I have been called by the Lord to write this book. People, especially pastors, need to be aware of the evil people who hide in their congregations. They need to know their plans and strategies against the church. If they are aware of the strategies, they can combat them effectively and give the church insight and wisdom on how to fight. I stood on the platform at church and looked directly at the programmers. I said, "There are evil people in every church with agendas against the church, but Papa God will expose them!" At that point, they got up and left the church. That was a great step against the enemy!

Chapter 16

Healing

"Then your light shall break forth like the morning, Your healing shall spring forth speedily, And your righteousness shall go before you; The glory of the LORD shall be your rear guard." Isaiah 58:8

There was a powerful group of people who started helping my spiritual papa with his prayer and deliverance ministry. We all were getting ministry, as well, to get the most healing possible. Wounded people, wound people, so it's very important for all of us to seek healing. There was a lady in particular who showed me Papa God's love in a powerful way. She sat in my ministry time and prayed while I was getting ministry. She gave me the first furniture of my own, a chair that was cushy and comfy. I would sit in that chair and talk with Papa God a lot. I even slept in the chair. This was a huge step for me, because I had never been allowed to actually sit on furniture. I always had to sit on the floor. It was so liberating for me! I didn't have to earn her acceptance. I called her "Amma," *mama* in the Indian culture.

All of us decided to go to the revival that was happening at the House of Prayer in Kansas City. The devil was trying to keep me from going. I got really sick before I went, but I knew I was supposed to go. When we got there, there was a great outpouring of joy at the revival. People were dancing, worshipping, and laughing. I was the only person on our team who wasn't able to feel joy at all. I couldn't figure out why everybody was joyful and I wasn't. I began to ask Papa God why I was so sad and unable to be joyful. He said that I felt guilty. The evil people named my daughter Joy. They gave me medicine that made me laugh, and then they began to hurt and kill her at the same time. They told me that I was evil because I was laughing at my daughter being hurt and killed. I couldn't stop laughing because the medication was forcing me to act in this way. I hated myself and wanted to die. They said to think about how evil I was when I saw joy (people laughing and happy). So every time I saw people laughing, worshipping, and looking happy, I thought of my little girl. I felt hideous and evil. At that moment there in the revival, Papa God gave me a vision of my little girl. She put my face in her hands and said, "It's okay to be happy, Momma. You don't have to be sad." I began to sob uncontrollably and was healed in that moment. For the rest of the revival, I laughed, worshipped, and danced! Papa God said, "All of heaven stops and watches me dance." There was another time that Papa God showed me a picture of Him with my little girl and my mom, who had been killed. I asked them, "Why can't I go be with you?" Papa God said it was because there were people that He would rescue through my story. If my testimony rescued one person, it is worth not giving up.

There were many times that Papa God would bring a memory to the surface where they told me I was evil, and then He would show me who I really was compared to who the evil people said I was. For example, they would say that I hated handicapped people and different races. Then the programmers would make something bad happen to them and say it was my fault. During my healing journey, Papa God has brought different races, ethnicity, and handicapped people into my life to love and show me who I really was. Every time something evil was happening, the programmers would say, "Be positive." That meant I had to forget. When Christians said, "Be positive," or "Think about what is good," I thought that meant someone was getting raped or tortured. Papa God began to heal me and show me the difference between being positive and denial. Being positive meant being honest about what Papa God is doing or what Papa God can do. Being positive did not mean you're supposed to pretend or deny the truth. This was also difficult when dealing with the faith confessions too. When I was sick, the programmers would say that I was faking it. They would say over and over that I wasn't sick, I was faking it. When I was crying, they would say I wasn't sad or in pain. Papa God is still healing me to understand how to be completely honest, and also how to genuinely believe at the same time. This was very confusing because of the programming.

The evil people showed up in the new town I was living in to intimidate and terrify me. Papa God caused me to be like the servant of Elisha in the scripture I shared previously. This has become one of my favorite scriptures. It shows the power of Papa God against our enemies! Second Kings 6:15–18 says, "When the servant of the man of God got up and went out early the next morning, an army with horses and chariots had surrounded the city. "Oh no, my lord! What shall we do?" the servant asked. 'Don't be afraid,' the prophet answered. 'Those who are with us are more than those who are with them.' And Elisha prayed, 'Open his eyes, Lord, so that he may see.' Then the Lord opened the servant's eyes, and he looked and saw the hills full of horses and chariots of fire all around Elisha. As the enemy came down toward him, Elisha prayed to the Lord, 'Strike this army with blindness.' So he struck them with blindness, as Elisha had asked." Papa God made them blind and unable to find me while they were there. They literally almost walked right past me while they were there, without even seeing me. He caused me to see that they weren't able to do anything to me because my mind wasn't under their control anymore.

When I initially got free, I was completely alone. I had no one. I was trying to protect the Christian couple and their family from the evil people. I didn't want them to get hurt any more than I had already hurt them. So I asked Papa God, "Who do You genuinely want me to love?" He brought to my mind the elderly ladies who were the Christian couple's adopted spiritual moms. These two ladies were sisters; their husbands had already passed away. I started going out to their house, spending time with them, and listening to their stories. I was doing whatever I could to show them love. This brought great healing for me because they didn't know anything about my past. They didn't know anything about my mistakes, so it was a clean slate for me. They just loved me, and I focused on them and loved them. This was also a way I could give back to the Christian couple for all of the things they had done for me. I had a lot of pain, guilt, and torment for all the pain I had caused them. I wasn't able to let my sins go. I kept beating myself up. I remember Papa God told me one day that being miserable wasn't doing anything for the Christian couple who rescued me. Genuinely living was the best way I could bless them for all that they had done for me. So I chose to let go of the condemnation that I had toward myself. The man had given me the scripture, "Therefore, there is now no condemnation for those who are in Christ." I began to focus, think, and pray about this scripture. It says there is no condemnation *now, not* after you beat yourself up enough.

One of the ladies got sick, and they put her in a nursing home. I would go pick up her sister and take her to the nursing home. This was a great joy! I began to see that maybe I wasn't evil and that I was capable of genuine love. Her sister ended up passing away; that was a great loss! I had for the first time really allowed my mind and spirit to love somebody without putting a wall up. I cried and sobbed when I lost her. When I was at the funeral, I saw the Christian couple who had given their life to genuinely give me freedom. They both told me that they forgive me. She told me that they pray for me. This was an awesome treasure to hear that they prayed for me. Papa God had also given me the name Beryl, from this beautiful lady who went to be with the Lord. It was her middle name. I will explain in detail about this a little later. This was another treasure that I would never forget. In my loss, He gave me a beautiful gift. During this time of loss, my amma (*mama* in Indian) gave me a necklace with an inscription that said, "I will carry you." Papa God knew that that was exactly what I needed to hear.

A couple of months later, my cat got sick for the third time with cancer. The first time she got sick, I had noticed she had a knot on her belly. My friend from church was a veterinarian. He said to bring her in. I found out she had cancer, and I had no money. I was so close to my cat; she was my family. She had been through a lot.

I had her when I was still getting programmed. They had used her to get to me. They tortured her, and the pain of having to watch that was more hideous than anything they could do to me. She was free now, but she had scars from the torture. Now after all that she had already been through, she was sick with cancer. The veterinarian and his wife from my church were so kind and loving. They did the surgery for free. She was so much better for a while, but then she got sick again, and another surgery had to be done. Again, they did the surgery for free! Papa God was really taking care of us. During the third time she got cancer, the veterinarian said she couldn't handle another surgery. I just couldn't let her go. I didn't want her to suffer, but I was afraid to give her up. I was praying and praying to have an idea when she was suffering and needed to be with Honest Jesus. She got so bad she wasn't even being able to walk and eat. She had a hole in her side from the cancer. I knew I had to stop the suffering. I just couldn't fathom seeing her die, though! Papa God showed me that I wasn't killing her by letting her go and ending her suffering. I took her to the vet, and I was sobbing the whole way there. I took her and held her, and Honest Jesus showed me that He walked into the room and put her in His arms. There was no pain for her any longer! She is running in heaven having so much fun!

Papa God gave me the verse in Habakkuk 2:2–3: "Then the LORD replied: 'Write down the revelation and make it plain on tablets so that a herald may run with it. For the revelation awaits an appointed time; it speaks of the end and will not prove false. Though it linger, wait for it; it will certainly come and will not delay.'" He gave me this verse over and over during my healing journey. I believe that His plan is to expose the evil people and bring millions out of darkness. I cling to this truth each day! I also believe that His Church will be awakened to the horrible evil that is happening in this country, and stand against it together in unity!

I still went to see the remaining sister after her other sister passed away. She needed me now more than ever. We were great friends and would talk for hours. I was terrified because when I visited her, I had to go back to the town that I had left when I became free. Every time I visited her, it was an ordeal. But I knew that Papa God was calling me to minister to her, so I went, choosing to trust that Papa God would take care of me.

I ended up getting my name legally changed because Papa God told me to. The name I had previously was a cult Illuminati name that I was tortured around. I had been praying for quite some time about what I should change my name to. I asked my elderly friend what her and her sisters' full names were. She told me that "Beryl" is a middle name of one of the ladies. It stood out to me, for some reason I didn't know. The next day, as I was reading the Bible, I opened my Bible to Song of Solomon 5:14: "His Hands are rods of gold set with beryl." Papa God said very clearly to me, "You are a precious gem. I have always had your spirit in My hand. This is your new name." Beryl is a precious gemstone. And Papa God had always had my spirit in His hand. This was a direct answer to the question I had asked Papa God, "Why didn't You protect me?" He said, "I wasn't able to protect your body because of the choices of evil people, but I always protected your spirit." No matter what they did to me, they could not destroy my spirit. So my last name was changed to Beryl legally. Hope was a name given to me by the Christian couple who had rescued me. I changed that legally as well. The entire name was a way of Papa God saying I was on an evil path that was chosen for me before, and now I was on Papa God's path. He also shared the verse about heaven with me: "The foundations of the city walls were decorated with every kind of precious stone. The first foundation was jasper, the second sapphire, the third agate, the fourth emerald, the fifth onyx, the sixth ruby, the seventh chrysolite, the eighth beryl, the ninth topaz, the tenth turquoise, the eleventh jacinth, and the twelfth amethyst." Eight means new beginning.

My elderly friend kept me from being lonely, and I helped ease the pain of the loss of her sister. She believed in me, and all she saw was somebody who had been kind and loving to her. She didn't see all of the rituals, rape, and torture. I went and visited with her every other week. We sang hymns (she played the piano) and talked about Papa God. She gave me a card that I still have. It's a picture of an old school house. She was a teacher when the school was a one room schoolhouse. The scripture on the card was 1 John 4:16. This is now my favorite verse. "And so we know and believe the love God has for us. God is love." I wrote her a poem about our time together, and when she passed away, I felt an intense loss.

At this point in my life, all of my support system in Kentucky was gone, and Papa God brought an opportunity for me to go to a ministry school in Tennessee. I spoke with the overseer of the supernatural school of ministry, and he said, "Sometimes God just wants us to make a choice to do something because we would like to do it." That advice sounded very liberating because I never thought Papa God would give me the ability to do something I wanted to do. So I told Papa God if he wanted me to go to the ministry school, then He would have to provide. So in a bittersweet gift, my friend who passed away left me just the amount of money I needed to go to the school. I quit my job, packed up, and moved to Tennessee on the day before my birthday six years ago. I was thirty-nine years old. I still talk to my spiritual papa a lot and other people I met there, but I haven't gone back to Kentucky. Kentucky is where most of the torture was done, so it brings many horrible memories. I miss my spiritual papa horribly, but he and his wife are doing very well.

There was intense warfare that happened with me leaving the state of Kentucky. A lot of territorial demons tormented me. I had the most intense pain in my head as I arrived in Tennessee, and we were trying to get our furniture unloaded. Then the warfare intensified as I began school! I began to learn more about the supernatural in a pure sense, not in the demonic realm. The devil was not happy that his territory was being destroyed. I genuinely felt the anointing flowing in all of the speakers that were brought in to teach our classes and conferences that were held there. I became great friends and family with the director of the school's wife, Wendy. She was kind and trustworthy, and she believed in me. He was the man I had talked with on the phone before I moved there, the main reason I ended up in Tennessee. They truly showed me what genuine family really is. Things don't have to be perfect in a family, but you're always there for each other. Papa God showed me that they didn't just say they were family; they really meant it. She and her husband provided an alternative that I needed to where I was living, so I moved in with them.

I had a beautiful bed with a white fluffy cover and soft pillow. They provided food that was actually good for my body, not fast food. She really taught me how to start taking care of my body and not feeding myself horrible food that destroyed my body. Even to this day, I have no doubts that if I needed somewhere to go, I would always be welcome at their house no matter what.

Every time we had worship before our ministry time and teaching in the ministry school, Papa God would bring up new memories and bring healing. Papa God showed me as we see our identity in who He says we are, the chains fall off, and we walk in our Kingdom Authority! I genuinely saw how His Presence brought healing. I used to hate worship and praise, because I was forced to have sexual feelings as the evil people played worship music. My programmers would say, "Just praise the Lord to get free." That meant that they would stimulate my genitals till I had an orgasm, and then they would tell me that I was an evil whore. I was so confused. I hated myself for having sexual feelings. I felt so out of control that I allowed my programmers to continue to torture me because I was terrified of myself and the sexual feelings. I was starting to get free from the fear of Papa God's presence through the ministry school in Tennessee, and He was bringing truth to root lies that kept me from genuine worship. There were many times when Papa God was showing me the memories of all the horror I went through. He showed me so many times that He was weeping and weeping over me for the pain I had to endure. There was one time in particular that I remember being in my car and screaming out from the pain of the things that I was seeing. I was seeing detail after detail of all that I had lived through. During this time, I saw a vision of Honest Jesus standing up for me, just like when He stood up for Steven, when he was being stoned. I will never forget that! There were many times where I screamed and cussed at Papa God because I was so angry about what they had done to me. He always allowed me to get those emotions out and then brought truth.

I began to see the gifts that Papa God put within my life, like prophecy, teaching, and preaching. Before I left for India, Papa God had told me that I was called to preach, and I never told anyone what He had shared with me. Then when we got to India, an Indian pastor who didn't even speak English spoke through a translator that I would be a mighty preacher. That was a great confirmation of Papa God's word!

Throughout my stay in ministry school, I received healing from the programming of perfection, coping with the habit of always trying to be good enough. I was asked to be the secretary of the church and school. The pastor and his wife were very kind and knew about some of the things I had endured. The programmers began to harass the pastor and his wife by sending letters saying they were loving parents who just wanted to see their daughter. They were trying to make me look crazy. They had always told me that they would make me look crazy if I ever tell anybody about what they did to me. The letters, phone calls, and packages were sent frequently. I was sad that my friends had to deal with this. I found out that there wasn't any way I could get a restraining order, since they had not physically harmed me recently. They showed up at church, and just like Papa God had promised. I was surrounded by His fire. I didn't even see them. My pastor's wife told them they had to leave, and they couldn't touch me! I was continually intimidated by letters and packages sent to me and all the people I was close to—no matter what I tried, even when I contacted a retired Navy SEAL who was investigating sex trafficking to stop the harassment. He was unable to do anything, as well as the police, because of the statute of limitations.

Papa God always reminds me that he will bring justice. That is His promise to me. Luke 8:17 says, "For all that is secret will eventually be brought into the open, and everything that is concealed will be brought into the light and made known to all." When I was in India the last time, when I was praying about exposing the evil people and the horror they did to me, our car drove by a sign at that exact moment that said, "Truth can't be hidden forever!" This was another assurance from Papa God that they will be exposed no matter what things look like. He has showed me over and over the scripture Psalm 23:5: "You prepare a table before me in the presence of my enemies." Papa God is blessing my life even as the evil people fight me constantly.

When I took the position of administrative assistant for the church, I met a lot of big-name Christian leaders. I felt like I had to try to impress them and like I was lesser in worth than all of them. I felt like I was the slave and everybody was important and I wasn't. There had been so much programming about the church. I thought that every Christian hated me and they wanted me dead. It was a long journey toward healing—to see the truth that we are all just people who are loved by Papa God. I'm still learning that each day. He has shown me that it's not my job to judge who is sincere and who isn't. He has gifted people in many different ways. If people are ministering on a stage, that doesn't mean they are prideful. They may be the most humble people and are just following Papa God in their calling. I had to go to the memories where the evil people made me feel like a dog and less than everybody else and allow Papa God to show me that being in ministry and being in the limelight does not make you important. The person who is cleaning the toilets is just as important as the person who is speaking on the stage. Through all of this healing time, I was distraught a lot, and the enemy was always trying to cause division with the people around me. I remember during Sunday school when a lady said something, and I thought she was mad at me. I left and went out to my car and cried. I called out to Papa God to get rid of all of the intense rejection I felt. He spoke clearly to me. "How can anybody say who you are? They didn't create you." So since He made me, only He can say who I truly am. That gave me a lot of comfort.

When I took the job with the church, I had a lot of difficulty with working at the church by myself during the day. This was a result of all the rituals that were done to me in churches, baptismal, altars, and sanctuaries. I would try to make myself focus on the job I was doing, but I would feel the anxiety and fear of what might happen to me there. Churches had never been a safe place for me. During the rituals, the programmers would put dead people on the altar and say that I have to save them and cover their sins. They would force me to do sexual things to them to bring them to life. Churches had always been torture chambers for me. To be saved meant that I had to have sex with Jesus, whomever they chose him to be. I was told that all of us were slaves to God, so we're chained up. They twisted the scripture Romans 6:22, "You have become slaves of God," and told me that God said I was His slave for life. Papa God showed me during my healing journey, the beauty of the real church. His real Church is His people.

I met a genuine example of the Church while I was going to missionary school to be ordained. I met the genuine family I wish I had always had since birth. There was a Christian couple who took me in as an adopted daughter. She was the mama I never had. She spoiled me and took me shopping. She was always in my corner. She helped me get my book published. Papa God used her in a mighty way! You never know how you are impacting a person's life when you step out and obey. I choose to trust Papa God. He will always give us back more than what we give!

Chapter 17

Walking in Freedom

"It is for freedom that Christ has set us free. Stand
firm, then, and do not let yourselves be burdened
again by a yoke of slavery." Galatians 5:1

It's so difficult to explain how paralyzing it is to have these intense memories surfacing all day long. I have chosen to live my life, though, no matter how difficult it is! The alternative is to just not get up each morning, but the evil people have already stolen too much of my life already. I choose to deal with all of the triggers and memories of thirty years of torture. I choose to live the life I was given by Papa God! At least this way, Papa God can rescue other people through my willingness to tell my story. The opportunity to plan conferences for this Christian ministry in Tennessee was healing for me because I got to see people being healed by Papa God in church instead of being tortured. It was such a powerful testimony of Papa God's genuine love.

While going to this church, I met a man named Daniel. He had moved to Tennessee the same year I did. He was given a prophetic word to leave Florida and move to Tennessee to pursue a music career. He gave up his six-figure income to follow Papa God to Tennessee. He was a hairstylist in Florida, and he was playing guitar in a worship band. Papa God gave him guitar as a child to connect with him through music. Daniel is an amazingly gifted musician. All the people who were close to me mentioned that he would be a good guy to be friends with and possibly date. He was in an extremely difficult situation in his life because he gave away everything he owned and left his flourishing business to move to Tennessee. He didn't have food to eat at times, and he was sleeping on the floor, in an apartment that was infested with mold. He was trying to do what he thought Papa God was telling him to do. I started praying about Daniel, and I saw a tree outside my window. Papa God said Daniel was like the tree. His roots went deep, but the fruit hadn't shown up yet. Papa God showed me you're only as strong as your foundation. Just like the roots of a tree, a skyscraper's foundation is laid below the ground to create the most stability. To get to the bedrock, it normally requires deep excavation of soils overlaying the bedrock. However, building the foundation on bedrock (Papa God) is necessary, given the extremely large loads of skyscrapers. When the bedrock (Papa God) is exposed, the massive foundation could be placed.

While I was getting ministry one day, I wasn't even thinking about Daniel, and Papa God gave me a vision. In my vision, Daniel was a little boy, and he was being told he wasn't good enough and that he was a loser. He was afraid and rejected, and he decided he never wanted to be close to people. He told himself that he wanted to be alone. Then I saw myself as a little girl. I was being hurt, and they were saying, "We don't want you. You're a loser." I was afraid of myself, and I was forced to be fearful if I didn't have people to keep me from being bad. We both were carrying fear and rejection. Then I saw Papa God, and He was riding in a new convertible with me. I was a little girl. Then I saw Daniel and myself in the car as little children with Jesus. From there, I saw us on a motorcycle with Honest Jesus. This ended up happening in the natural not long after that. I got a convertible with which Daniel and I went on lots of rides in the country, and we felt Papa God's presence. Daniel got a motorcycle, and we went riding, and I talked to Papa God the entire time. A little later, Daniel traded in that motorcycle, and he bought a Harley Davidson Road Glide. The motorcycle was too expensive, and we wanted to begin to save for a wedding. So he asked for Papa God to take the motorcycle from him because he couldn't afford it. That same week, someone stole the motorcycle, and his gap insurance paid for all of it except the down payment. This was testimony that Papa God is always working on our behalf.

At this point, it was the end of 2014, and Papa God showed me that He was going to establish a ministry specifically for exposing the truth of what I had been through. Papa God rescued me out of that hell, and He wanted to encourage others that He can rescue anybody from anything. I was living proof that He is big enough to heal the deepest pain, and not only heal it, but provide an abundant life afterward! Papa God shared that this was the time to move on from the church I had been at. There was something new He wanted to do! He shared with me He wanted me to have the freedom to share all of my story, and not be connected with any ministry so that I could share all of the things that He had asked. So I stepped away and got a job waitressing. This was a difficult time due to financial reasons, and I was unable to find a job. I kept asking Papa God to intervene, and He always provided for my needs. I made many mistakes as I learned how to live for the first time, but Papa God was always there!

Daniel had been praying about an engagement ring to give me. He went into place that had an antique store and different businesses, and there was a church there. He went to look at guitars, and while he was looking, he heard an angelic sound. It was from the worship music playing. He decided to go into the church service, and they were talking about marriage. He stopped by the antique store on the way out, and the ring he had been asking Papa God for was there. He had worked out all of the details. On Christmas day, Daniel gave me my presents, and I was disappointed that I didn't get a ring. Then he said, "Look in that stocking." The stocking was the one the Christian couple made for me. It was very special to me. I looked into the stocking, and there was my ring. Papa God gave me the gift of Jesus on Christmas, and He gave me my husband as well! The journey in our relationship has not been easy. There have been intense attacks on our marriage from the evil people, but we have had great healing along the way. The couple we met at church and who adopted me threw us a beautiful wedding. I walked down the aisle to "You Raised Me Up." This was the favorite song of the man who had the most to do with rescuing me from slavery. So I played it as a tribute to him and my freedom.

I had been unable to find someone to minister to me when I moved to Tennessee. It is extremely difficult to find Christians who minister to SRA and mind-control survivors. That is another reason why Papa God had me write this book. Papa God is calling His children to minister and pray for people who are trying to get out of what I went through. Unfortunately, it is difficult to even find Christians who believe that this type of mind control exists. It's hard for people to comprehend that there is that level of evil. There is a very real devil, and there are people who follow him.

I was referred to a man who had a Christian counseling ministry. I began going to ministry weekly. Papa God brought healing and truth during this time. The minister ended up getting cancer and passing away. He was an amazing man. During the programming, I had been told over and over that I was the cause of every person's death. When the minister died, I thought this was another case where I was the reason for bad things that happen to people. Even after getting free, I had Christians say they couldn't be around me because there was too much of a demonic battle. So I had a lot of rejection. Papa God showed me it was not my fault for the evil that was done by the Illuminati and the programmers, and even the warfare was their fault not mine. Little by little, I don't blame myself for things anymore. Papa God said "just like a sunrise doesn't have to try to be beautiful, it just is, that's the way His creation is. We are His creation! Jeremiah 33:3 ³'Call to me and I will answer you and tell you great and unsearchable things you do not know.'

Throughout my healing journey for the last thirteen years, I have been through the training and ministry of Sozo, Freedom Encounters, Transformation Ministries, In His Steps, School of the Supernatural, Rapha Christian Ministries, and Daniel Duval Ministries. I have completed twenty-four plus Beth Moore studies; Priscilla Shirer, Shannon Ethridge, and other woman's ministries; numerous conferences; and three years of ministry school with Christian leaders and speakers. All of this just to get healing and deliverance and to be able to live my life without torment and terror. I don't say this to say that

I'm responsible for my healing in anyway or to be prideful. I only say this to motivate people to see that we have to partner with Papa God to allow His healing to take place in our lives. He will not force His Way into my life or force me to allow Him to heal me. My only job is to make the choice to allow healing. I have a Papa God-given fight to not allow the evil people to take my life from me any longer, I will partner with Papa God to take down the enemy no matter what. To rescue the weak and enslaved till the last breath in my body. Ephesians 5:11 says, "Have nothing to do with the fruitless deeds of darkness, but rather expose them." Are you willing to join the fight? I pray that you are, because survivors need you. We need you to see the truth and step up to allow Papa God to use your life to believe us, expose the evil, and fight against it. Prayer is one way that you can change things. If you can't gather enough compassion for me, think if this was your daughter, son, brother, sister, husband, wife…What would you be willing to do for them?

Papa God has genuinely promised me that millions will be set free. The genuine promises of Papa God are ours. Even if we don't see them, we have to trust that Papa God is working. It's what we focus on. When we lasso and the rope goes over the horse's neck, that horse is ours. So whatever we focus and pull to us is ours from Papa God. During my healing, I would look up and see a person parachuting, and Papa God said that genuinely trusting Him is like parachuting. You stand at the edge of the cliff and jump. A big area of healing that needed to take place was dealing with self-hatred. This healing happened day after day. I was learning that continual self-rejection is an open invitation to Satan. It was important for me to see this and stand against it. In what I said and how I treated myself, I began to learn to be kind to myself. I'm still healing daily. First Peter 5:8 says, "Be alert and of sober mind. Your enemy the devil prowls around like a roaring lion looking for someone to devour."

During my healing journey, sometimes, I would push and push to see the memories out of works. I had been programmed to always see the evil in myself, and if I wasn't seeing the evil within myself, I must be doing something horrible. The evil people used this programming against the ministry in Kentucky with the Christian couple. They had already gotten their manual of ministry and studied it and found a way to twist the ministry so it would not be effective. The evil people said instead of the ministry revealing the truth that I was a pure child of Papa God that the ministry was just there to trick me and show me the evil within me over and over. So every time I would get ministry, I would think I was getting tricked into exposing how evil I was. It was excruciating. They used this to program me against the Christian couple and the ministry that they were doing. To this day, I still get terror and fear before I get ministry. I do experience tremendous pain during my ministry, but it's pain that has been within me for decades. The ministry is allowing the pain to surface and be destroyed, while Papa God brings truth to replace the lies I was told. The momentary pain of this healing is a million times better than having pain for the rest of my life. Once the memory is healed and truth is brought from Papa God to the lies, I never have to see those things again. It is 100 percent finished. Also, as I get free, I'm able to have an abundant life that had been stolen from me before.

For the past ten years, Papa God has been asking me to write this book. He said to not to leave anything out. The evil people still try to intimidate, manipulate, and control me by showing up at my jobs. By showing up at my husband's work, by sending mail and pictures. But I refuse to back down, and I chose to tell the entire truth of what they did to me. Now is the time. Esther revealed who she was, even though she was in danger. "For such a time as this" (Esther 4:14). Just as Haman planned her destruction, Papa God reversed Haman's plan and reversed all of Satan's plan, for Esther's destiny to be brought forth. "Whoever digs a hole and scoops it out falls into the pit they have made. The trouble they cause recoils on them; their violence comes down on their own heads" (Psalm 7:15–16).

There is scripture after scripture that shows what Papa God says about evil men. Psalm 34:16 says, "The face of the LORD is against evildoers, to cut off the memory of them from the earth." Isaiah 31:2 says, "Yet He also is wise and will bring disaster and does not retract His words, but will arise against the house of evildoers, and against the help of the workers of iniquity." In Isaiah 42:13, it says, "The

Lord shall go forth like a mighty man; He shall stir up His zeal like a man of war. He shall cry out, yes shout aloud; He shall prevail against His enemies."

As I write this, there are racial wars, political wars, and terrorist attacks all over the world. There are Illuminati elites who are orchestrating these attacks to cause a war so that they can bring martial law into place. If they can get the country divided, then they can bring it down. I believe Papa God has raised up President Trump as a *trump card* to destroy the Illuminati's plans and unite this country for Papa God. I call all Christians to pray together for the truth to be exposed about the Illuminati. "Behold, I send you forth as sheep in the midst of wolves: be ye therefore wise as serpents, and harmless as doves" (Matthew **10:16**). That we would pray for each other and the destruction of the New World Order. Also, that President Trump will be aware of their tactics and will be backed in prayer to expose them.

Lance Wallnau has been criticized extensively, but he has been a major force in exposing how Papa God brought Trump into office and the battle that he is fighting against the elite. The recent candidate and her husband have been a force behind childhood pedophilia for decades, and they are gathering her victims from all countries, especially the United States. When she chose her election day venue at the glass-enclosed auditorium, she was saying to the victims that her evil was shielded by all the people she is paying off to keep her secrets, the invisible shield of protection by those elites close to her. There will be a day in eternity that she will not be able to hide her evildoing. Everything will be exposed for all to see.

Another area that Papa God has been sharing truth about is the direct correlation between electrical waves and demons. All demons ride on electrical waves. With the current electronic age, this means that every time we use our phones, watch TV, etc., we are opening ourselves up and submitting ourselves to the electronic waves of these devices. This does not mean that watching TV or talking on the phone is wrong, in any way. It just means that we have to be wise and cover ourselves in prayer before submitting to what is going on in our environment. Take Facebook for example, it is the motherboard of our electronic system in this country, gathering information 24/7.

The government and elite can track what you like, dislike, what time you get up, go to sleep, go to eat, on and on…How do you take down your enemy? You study every detail about them. Every weakness is picked apart to strategically bring them to ruin without them ever being aware that they are fighting against anyone. That is what Hitler did. His reign was planned for years and years before he took over Germany. Daily, he desensitized them to what he was doing bit by bit, and before they knew it, they were no longer free. Even dreams are manipulated through electronic impulses. The evil people do rituals and act out the dream, then scan a picture of the person they want to turn you against, apply the picture of the person's face on top of their face, then summon the demons to transmit the dream to the electrical waves during REM sleep cycle. If the person has already been opened up to demonic spirits, then an access point and portal is open for them to transmit the dream. Ever since I became free, I have had nightmare night after night—dreams so specific I knew that they were sent by the Illuminati. Papa God showed me that there were portals and access points opened up by the Illuminati during my sleep. I pray specifically for Papa God to stand guard over those portals and access points. And I pray against any electronic messages being sent while I sleep.

As a child, I was hooked up to a telephone with sensors. They scanned my female programmer and downloaded electrical impulses into the left part of my body. They placed an electrode in my temple and jaw. This was planted within my body to make a connection electronically to their computer systems. The electrode in my temple was the receiver, so I could receive the electrical impulses and messages by Morse code that they wanted me to get. The electrode in my jaw was the transmitter. It was used to send message back to them about my location and what I was doing every second. The left side of my body was planted with DNA from my female programmer to cause a soul tie and legal right for the demons to bond to those electrodes. The evil people told me that I was a cyborg taken from her and that I was a replica of her. This is terrifying because I was told that I was no more than a robot made from her DNA. So this set up a double bind of denial in my mind. I wanted to be like her because then I was told I would be real. But I didn't want to be like her because she was hideously evil. So in order to be real and to connect to people they tortured me to believe I had to be evil. This was a double bind because as a human being one of our basic needs is to connect and bond with others. This was used as another method to cause me to cling to my torturer and programmer.

The right side of my body, they called the denial side. I was told that DNA of my programmer was injected in my bloodstream to cause me to be a clone of her. So if I viewed my programmer as evil, that meant I had to view myself as evil. This was done to ensure that I never told anybody the truth about what they were doing to me. If I told anybody, then I would actually be telling people about myself being evil. They would twist this even further by telling me that I wasn't even real and that I was programmed as a robot and clone to kill whomever they forced me to kill. They said they tried to rescue me, but they couldn't so they injected me with their DNA to try and save me. They said I was the root of all evil. I was terrified when I wasn't being tortured and manipulated, and I begged to not be left alone. My fear was that I would be a robot that killed people all the time. During my ministry time, Papa God showed me that my emotions were evidence that I was not a robot or clone. A clone or robot would not have emotions; tears were able to be replicated but not the true emotions that Papa God created. If you do any google search on cloning and artificial intelligence, there are more signs of the truth that is hidden by the elite and the military starting to surface. The reason for this is that they have desensitized the American people into believing this is normal, and nothing to be concerned about. This has been going on for decades, all under the surface and disguise of a free nation. There are more slaves than ever before in our nation.

A specific actor is at the top of the mountain of entertainment in the Illuminati. His movies have been used to program all victims of Illuminati mind control. Starting with *The Truman Show*, Truman was in the Illuminati, and an Illuminati programmer. This movie shows how they program victims to be under their control every second of every day with an outside presenter part that has no idea they are being controlled. It also shows a control room, which controls the winds and airwaves in Truman's world. Then the movie *Bruce Almighty*, where a person is God. In all of the rituals, he is God, and he controls what clones and artificial programming is inserted within the victims. He is at the top of the experiments of mind control and how the brain works, creating actors out of victims. In another movie, he talks about part of the rituals, telling them they will be victims of the claw if they do not act and pretend. The claw is the connector to the real world through electrocution and electrical implants, through which they control victims with daily. The Mask is the denial world they created by making each victim wear a mask that electrocutes them if they do not pretend and act like their programmers are good. These movies are used to bury all memories of who this actor is and what he is really doing.

Chapter 18

Exposing the Darkness

"Behold, I will make those of the synagogue of Satan who say that they are Jews and are not, but lie—behold, I will make them come and bow down before your feet and they will learn that I have loved you." Revelation 3:9

Now I go and speak at every opportunity to share about the truth of sex trafficking. This is a great passion of mine to set the captive free. Sex trafficking is a small piece of what the Illuminati does, but if I can't get people to believe that there are sex trafficking victims here in the southern part of the United States, how will I ever get them to believe and fight with me against the evil Illuminati mind control? During one of my ministry times, I was weeping loudly at the depth of my being because of the sadness I felt that people did not believe the truth about what millions of people are enduring here in the US. Jesus showed me that He was weeping too and that He is very sad that people do not believe, especially His people. He said that they do not know. They have been deceived and have been clouded in their vision. Throw off the clouds and deception of denial brought by the enemy, and chose to see the truth of what is happening in this nation. The freedom of millions of people depends upon it! The freedom of your children depends upon it. Your freedom depends upon it.

There were so many times that Papa God brought an avalanche of healing through a word or a small thing that I never would have thought He would use to heal me. I was at a women's conference called the Ball in the Fall. I went to the restroom, and I couldn't get the toilet paper off of the roll, I was annoyed, and I finally tore a jagged piece of toilet paper off. Papa God said, "This is like healing. It's not perfect. It's a little at a time, jagged and torn, but I will heal all of you a little at a time. Papa God can use the smallest things and normal everyday things to speak to us. Papa God went on to say this is how you are qualified to speak to other people. You are not perfect. You are in process just like every other person." This showed me that He will bring up every lie and memory in His Timing in His way, and He will flush all of those lies down the toilet, never to return. After that, there was a little girl about three or four years old with a pretty dress and tiara on, sitting in front of me; and she turned around, smiled, and showed me her tiara. At that moment, Papa God said, "Those parts of yourself that you were told are monsters, werewolves, vampires, and pure evil, I see them just like I see this little girl." My view of myself changed in that moment, and I began to cry. I was just a little girl with a beautiful dress and tiara, the royalty of Papa God, even at the deepest darkest part of my being. Papa said, "If that little girl asked for something to eat, would you give her things that you knew would kill her, or would you give her things that were going to strengthen her and bring her life?" At that moment, I knew that I had been feeding my body things that I knew would kill me, and that I had been doing that because I wanted to kill those parts of myself. Feeding your body well is loving yourself and being kind to yourself.

Another revelation Papa God brought about my identity happened when I was working through a memory with some amazing friends that I have. They minister to many SRA survivors. During that ministry, Papa God showed me He was digging a jewel out of the sand on a beautiful beach. When He got to the jewel, the jewel shone so bright I was blinded. The stone was green like beryl. He said that the jewel was me. I was shining brightly just because that is who I was created to be, not because I did anything. A jewel just shines! Then He showed me the evil people taking the jewel and sanding it, throwing it, stomping it, and burying it. That is what the evil people were doing to me. They were trying to bury and destroy who I genuinely was created to be. This brought great healing! At that point, He showed me paintings on the wall that a friend of mine had painted, and He said that that was true beauty. The paintings would not be especially spectacular to people who looked at the surface for beauty, but for people who choose to look deep to see the genuine beauty. They were extraordinarily beautiful. He sees the genuine beauty within us. He sees the colors and creativity and passions. He sees who we really are. My friends have the gift of seeing the beauty that Papa God sees that other people do not. When looking at survivors and victims of satanic ritual abuse and government-sponsored mind control, you have to look past the outside programming and see who Papa God truly formed them to be. This will get you through the depth of the programming, anger, rage, hate, and demonic activity that has been programmed into them to cover up the genuine person created by Papa God!

As I write this book, I'm learning what rest genuinely is meant to be. The evil people programmed me to believe that I would only have rest when I watched TV. I was told this was because they could connect to my mind through the electrical waves and control me. So my entire life, I have been addicted to watching TV. Even though I wanted to do other things, I was driven to watch TV so that I would be controlled. This was the only fake rest that I had. I always felt drained and depressed after watching TV, but I didn't know how to stop. My healing has been layer by layer. So I would get freedom, and then another area would be exposed; then I would fall into watching TV constantly again. This was driven by intense fear and terror. The terror carried electrical currents too. And until I began to address all of the sources of energy attacking me, I was fighting a losing battle. The lady who ministers to me wrote a prayer that Papa God gave her, called the energy-blocking prayer. Since praying that prayer for the first time in my life, I have not had any compulsion to watch TV!

The encouraging part of healing is that once an area is healed by Papa God, that area never again has to be visited. It is over! When we settle with keeping our pain and woundedness, we keep the wounds for a lifetime, and the pain continues. That's why I encourage every single person to seek healing; healing brings abundant life from the hand of Papa God. I don't want to settle for anything other than an authentic life.

Another area of false rest that was programmed into me was eating fast food and sugary foods. If I wanted to make sure I didn't sin, I was tortured to believe that I had to feed myself things that hurt my body. These types of things exist in every person's life, just not to this degree of being programmed to make those choices. The enemy programs people to believe that certain things—whether it's drugs, Facebook, food, or whatever—are the answer for finding rest and peace from our pain. The only rest from pain is a true genuine connection with Papa God. No counterfeit will do what the presence of Papa God will do to bring rest. As I was writing this, I heard Papa God say, now genuinely rest, so automatically my mind went to going to my house and watching TV. Then I thought, you know, I feel at rest now. I was at a place of connection and communion with Papa God. He always teaches us something new every second of every day if we listen.

Another way the evil people connect remotely to victims are through sensors that are put in the body, close to the heart, brain, or other essential organs. The working of the organs creates algorithms that transmit to sensors, and the sensors communicate with the receptors that they have in their satellite system and computers. This is already being done with organ transplants. Hospitals use algorithms to locate the organs of people who need a transplant the most. This has been done for many years, but now people are desensitized to the moral and ethical issues this brings. The evil people use the sensors to scramble the signals so that it makes it feel almost impossible to connect to anybody because of the static and confusion in the atmosphere. There is a literal matrix that is put in place to cause confusion. Then demons are funneled through the rabbit hole or portal. This is what is shown in the movie the *Matrix*. Most sci-fi movies are based on some form of programming. This causes the American people to be desensitized to the truth that there are people who are being tortured, manipulated, and controlled every day. The evil people use encryption keys to keep the mind from going to specific information that is held in the unconscious. This is demonically set up through ritual sacrifice.

There is so much interference with the spirit realm through the electrical wavelengths that the evil people send; it is very difficult to communicate with Papa God. When I take a bath or shower, the static is reduced significantly, because tap water is not conductive. I can talk with Papa God during this time and feel like I'm not warring the entire time. During the times of war, the promise of Psalms 1 is what I cling to.

> Blessed is the one who does not walk in step with the wicked or stand in the way that sinners take or sit in the company of mockers, but whose delight is in the law of the LORD, and who meditates on his law day and night. That person is like a tree planted by streams of water, which yields its fruit in season and whose leaf does not wither—whatever they do prospers. Not so the wicked! They are like chaff that the wind blows away. Therefore the wicked will not stand in the judgment, nor sinners in the assembly of the righteous. For the LORD watches over the way of the righteous, but the way of the wicked leads to destruction.

Even as we speak, I'm getting e-mails from the programmers. The e-mails contain hidden messages to me such that when a Christian looked at it, they look as though they are loving kind parents. I have been told by Christians, "Why don't you just sit down with them and work things out?" This infuriates me, because they have no idea about the level of evil that these people are operating in; they are taken over by evil completely. Not only do they choose Satan willingly with knowledge of the Word and who Papa God is. They gave their entire creation over to Satan to be used for whatever, whenever, and however. There is no limit to the evil that can be done through a person who has given up their created body of the Almighty Papa God over to Satan. They have made their choice.

The most recent e-mail I received from the programmers was about Yom Kippur, the day of atonement. To Christians and other people looking with their natural eyes, this is just an innocent e-mail. But to a victim who has been tortured around Yom Kippur and forced to be used as an atonement for other people's sins, this is a message of terror. Also, the day of atonement was used to make us turn against Papa God, and they would say that he required "us," the people with mixed breed status, to find another way of atonement. He refused to die or atone for our sins. Papa God in my healing process showed me that His blood flows through my veins; ultimately, He is the source of all DNA and bloodlines. People have a difficult time accepting this because they put such emphasis on genetic and biological family, and that is important, but spiritual family is the most important and the source of all real family that is above all other family. If we could as the body of Christ begin to see things in this light, we would have much more compassion and unity in the church. Instead of fighting against each other, we would see that we are all brothers and sisters in Christ. We are a family that will be together for eternity. Why shouldn't we have each other's backs? Why shouldn't we encourage each other and support each other?

Currently, the last form of harassment has been a threat to sue me. I did an online interview, and the programmers contacted the lady who interviewed me. They intimidated and threatened to sue. They continue to send e-mails and use other victims to try and manipulate me to be quiet. They had a victim donate to my ministry with a specific amount that was donated that triggered deep memories. For example, five dollars was donated, and they had told me that if I ever told anybody about what they were doing, they would eliminate me. The number five was the number of people in the house where I was enslaved. There were two programmers, and two other victims, plus myself. The five would be brought to four, when they killed me. In rituals, they would torture me and say that they had removed me from the five. Then they would put me in a cage and act like they didn't see me. I didn't exist. So now they are trying to silence me because they know I'm talking. If I don't say something, who will? If I don't stand up, who will? I refuse to sit around and play things safe when other people are dying and being tortured every day. That is not who Papa God created me to be.

How about you? Are you going to live a comfortable life, or the life that Papa God intended for you to live? Because that life will bring peace but not comfort. He is always pushing us out of our comfort zones to grow and to soar higher. He has great things for us if we step out of our comfort and choose to listen to His voice and follow His plan. He may be saying to you, "This is real. Believe this," and your mind is saying there is no way this could have really happened. Ask Papa God to show You what voice to listen to. Satan will always try to use our logical mind against us, but our logical mind is a gift from Papa God. It's the lies that the enemy uses against us that try to distort our logical mind. That is why it takes genuine faith to walk with Papa God, to see past the natural into the spiritual. I pray that every Christian will begin to walk in the Spirit and listen to Papa God's voice. He is crying out for us to be free. Will you hear Him please?

About the Author

Hope Beryl-Green is a speaker, author, and founder of There Is Freedom Ministries. Hope survived thirty years of sex slavery, satanic ritual abuse, and government-sponsored mind control. Hope lives an abundant life now, and she is passionate about telling her story—as well as inspiring others to know they can be rescued too. She daily reminds people that there is no wound too deep or bondage too big that Papa God can't free them. Hope has been the keynote speaker for colleges, airport police, community and nonprofit groups, and numerous TV appearances. The knowledge and insight she possesses will transform the view of freedom in this culture.

Lightning Source UK Ltd.
Milton Keynes UK
UKHW011056200720
366842UK00002B/387